Out of the Past

Books by Barry Gifford

FICTION
Wyoming
The Sinaloa Story
Baby Cat-Face
Arise and Walk
Night People
Port Tropique
Landscape with Traveler
A Boy's Novel
My Last Martini

THE SAILOR AND LULA NOVELS
Wild at Heart
Perdita Durango
Sailor's Holiday
Sultans of Africa
Consuelo's Kiss
Bad Day for the Leopard Man

NONFICTION
Bordertown (with David Perry)
The Phantom Father: A Memoir
A Day at the Races
Out of the Past: Adventures in Film Noir
The Neighborhood of Baseball
Saroyan: A Biography (with Lawrence Lee)
Jack's Book: An Oral Biography of Jack Kerouac (with Lawrence Lee)

POETRY
Flaubert at Key West
Ghosts No Horse Can Carry
Giotto's Circle
Beautiful Phantoms
Persimmons: Poems for Paintings
The Boy You Have Always Loved
Poems from Snail Hut
Horse hauling timber out of Hokkaido forest
Coyote Tantras
The Blood of the Parade
Selected Poems of Francis Jammes (translations, with Bettina Dickie)

PLAYS
Hotel Room Trilogy

SCREENPLAYS
Lost Highway (with David Lynch)

Out of the Past

Adventures in *Film Noir*

Barry Gifford

University Press of Mississippi / Jackson

Revised edition

Published and expanded in 2001 by University Press of Mississippi

Originally published by Grove Press in 1988 under the title *The Devil Thumbs a Ride & Other Unforgettable Films*.

Many of these essays originally appeared in *Projections* (London), *San Francisco Bay Guardian*, and *Mystery Scene*.

www.upress.state.ms.us

09 08 07 06 05 04 03 02 01   4 3 2 1

Library of Congress Cataloging-in-Publication Data

Gifford, Barry, 1946–

    Out of the past : adventures in film noir / Barry Gifford.

      p. cm.

      1. Film noir—United States—Reviews. I. Title.

PN1995.9.F54 G54 2000

791.43'655—dc21   00-023947

British Cataloging-in-Publication Data available

This book is for Phoebe Gifford, who knows a good movie when she sees one. Remember: even though life isn't black and white, it often looks better that way.

Love,
Daddy

"Never argue with the movies."
—Frank O'Hara

Introduction

To most students of film the movies dealt with here are properly called *noir*, which might be loosely translated as "of the night." But considering that the movies range from the rather loopy psychosis of *The Devil Thumbs a Ride* to the melancholic doom of the title film, it's obvious that *noir* is handy as a catch-all but useless as a definition. So let us forget definitions and simply enjoy this most fascinating book on films about corruption and crime in all its varieties, from the lyric beauty of *Badlands* to the pitiless precision of *Charley Varrick*.

If you grew up in the '50s you were told that art was to be judged by its intentions. Films and books with "important" themes were almost automatically viewed as important works. (Has anybody tried to struggle through *The War Lover*, book or film, lately?) Films and books about crime almost never found themselves in that category. Although art is generally found in brows high or low, but rarely in middle, nobody knew that yet.

Only during the cultural revisionism of the '60s (which had some low as well as high points, considering the celebration of, say, rock lyrics as real poetry) was an intelligent eye turned to crime movies. There were four decades of talkies to assess and reassess and the work was done by good people such as Andrew Sarris and Roger Ebert and later Janet Maslin, with great high seriousness but almost no academic flapdoodle. Critics learned that accessibility was important not only on the screen but on the page as well.

Gradually we began to understand that some great and near-great movies had been pushed from sight by a critical establishment bloated on Hollywood hype or academic arrogance. By the time *Cape Fear*, for example, appeared in 1962, it was almost immediately recognized as a classic American film. The same could be said for *Chinatown* and *Body Heat*. You had to be pretty foolish to misunderstand how powerful and important these films were.

But the real chore was unearthing all those movies that had been virtually and in some cases literally lost, *Detour* being a good example. It's not hard to understand why most people would consider *Detour* interesting trash at best. It is not, in many respects, a good film. Its plot depends almost exclusively on coincidences (one right after the other), the dialogue is strictly spear-carrier stuff (just advance the plot, boys) and some of the camera set-ups are so haphazard they have the look of the cheapest porn.

All that said, *Detour* remains a masterpiece of its kind. There have been hundreds of better movies, but none with the feel for doom portrayed by director Edgar G. Ulmer. The random universe Stephen Crane warned us about—the berserk cosmic impulse that causes earthquakes and famine and AIDS—is nowhere better depicted than in the scene where Tom Neal stands by the roadside, soaking in the midnight rain, feeling for the first time the noose drawing tighter and tighter around his neck.

It is a long way from Tom Neal to Robert Mitchum. Mitch was all the things Neal wasn't, and that meant he was usually able not only to make sense of the endless night but to impose his will on it. Neal and Mitchum represent the opposite ends of *noir:* Neal the sweaty trapped animal, Mitchum the cool if angry man after both answers and dignity. (Which is why his performance as Phillip Marlowe in *Farewell, My Lovely* is the definitive interpretation of Marlowe.)

The movies discussed here range from the lowest of the Bs to the biggest of the As, and this book is going to make you want to run out and locate every one of them (and good luck to you; finding *The Devil Thumbs A Ride* could take a lifetime). Through Barry Gifford's eyes we begin to see their similarities and their value. What Sarris did for the mainstream film in *The American Cinema*, Barry does here for the crime film.

Barry is not strictly speaking a critic (and this book is not in any formal way criticism) but rather a novelist and cultural observer who has written well and variously about the American scene of his times. He brings to these pages his gifts—tapped-out humor, dignified anger, an ear for the subtlest and most valuable kind of gossip—that can illuminate not only the movies but also our own experience. This book will show you what's been going on in this country the past four decades. These writers and directors and actors and actresses (take particular note of Ida Lupino) insisted on talking about the culture not as it should be or we'd like it to be, but as it was. They were purveyors of sometimes difficult and bleak truths, and like all such people they were rarely applauded for their troubles; indeed, they were held in a kind of contempt by their more suntanned peers.

Film noir, however you choose to define it, is inexorably American, even when the Brits get hold of it (as in the vastly underappreciated *Get Carter*), and that is what Barry understands most of all, that *noir* is the cinematic fever chart of the American dream in this century, from the doomed teenagers of *Rebel Without a Cause* to the middle-class concerns of *Mildred Pierce.*

This is a book of very special gifts, some of which will enlighten, some of which will provoke, all of which bring you the joy of encountering a formidable intelligence and a look at our country and times that you probably haven't encountered before.

—Edward Gorman and Dow Mossman

Ace in the Hole

(also known as *The Big Carnival*) 1951. Directed by Billy Wilder. Starring Kirk Douglas, Jan Sterling, Richard Benedict, Robert Arthur and Porter Hall.

The bronc bucked on the red Wyoming license plate as the battered purple pickup carrying two men in black cowboy hats lurched along the highway past the outskirts of Albuquerque. I followed close behind, wondering where in wide-open Wyoming they were from and what they were doing this far from home. An empty beer bottle rolled off the back of the open truck tailgate and crashed just ahead of my maroon '55 Buick Century, crunching under the right front tire.

I decided to try and pass the pickup and see what these two boys looked like. It was a two-lane, and after topping a rise I swung the Buick out to the left into the opposite lane and stabbed it. When I pulled even with the pickup cab I slowed a moment and stole a look. They were two old fellas, looked like they just tumbled in off the range, jagged sideburns, beards half-full, lean and wiry, in their late fifties, sixties-and-some, both grim-mouthed and eyes set to the sunset blue-red road in front of them. I moved the Buick past, taking a curve sharper than I should have, tires squealing, leaving the old boys behind.

I decided to stop for coffee at a cafe west of town. I sat at the counter. There were two other customers in the place, an old man and an Indian kid, both of whom sat at the far end of the long side of the L-shaped counter eating chili out of dark blue enamel bowls. The old man did not look up while he ate. The Indian kid glanced over at him every few seconds to see that the old man was doing all right.

Then the angel appeared. I was sure she was an angel, an omen, a fawn-child no more than thirteen years old in a white waitress uniform, platinum hair tied tight to her head, clear blue eyes surrounded by an inky path of make-up, Lolita-like with skirt stopped top of the thigh and disdainful lip no doubt dealt with midnight truckers, small town wifely sneers, all men mad to unwrap and sup at the sweet sap purity tap. But there was so much coldness, hardness in her stare that I had to avert my eyes, blink blindly at the menu, then gaze again, unable to convince myself that this was no vision, no lie, but the pearl of New Mexico.

I couldn't help but follow her movements carefully, and didn't dare look away when she bent to retrieve a fallen utensil, revealing the underside of her thighs and flash of flame-pink cotton. I coughed and she brought me a glass of water. I ordered coffee and scrambled eggs and toast.

Outside again I spat out the window and drove on, leaving the angel of the desert cafe to her Hollywood dreams, to age, to what I couldn't touch but what I could not help but be touched by.

Algiers

1938. Directed by John Cromwell. Screenplay by John Howard Lawson with additional dialogue by James M. Cain. Starring Charles Boyer, Hedy Lamarr, Sigrid Gurie, Joseph Calleia, Alan Hale and Gene Lockhart.

This is a remake of *Pepe le Moko*, the French classic that starred Jean Gabin as a gangster sequestered in the Casbah, from which he controls a network of criminals. In English, it's Charles Boyer as Pepe. The French police come to Algiers determined to apprehend Pepe, suggesting a house to house search, at which the Algerians scoff. Joseph Calleia plays the native cop who actually hangs out at Pepe's and tells him he'll get him one day. But Pepe is protected in the Casbah maze—anyone who means him harm would never get out of there alive.

Scripted by one of the Hollywood Ten with clean-up work by a master of American menace, *Algiers*'s premise is that Pepe is tired of life behind the walls, even though he has money, women and power. The French want him back for crimes he's committed there, and the Algiers police have no recourse but to wait him out. Sooner or later, Calleia knows, something will lure him from his stronghold. Of course, it turns out to be a woman, Miss Hedy Lamarr, straight from her Czechoslovakian *Ecstasy*, wherein she appeared topless and caused a sensation. In truth, her body wasn't so great but her face was exquisite. She was one of the all-time great beauties of the 1930s and '40s. She's with a group of tourists when Pepe meets her, and the suave Boyer, in black shirt and white tie, is immediately captivated. Her name is Gaby, and she is intrigued by this slick, powerful figure, the notorious Pepe le Moko, living legend of The Casbah.

Pepe has a main squeeze, Sigrid Urie, who becomes insanely jealous, and conspires with the lackey Gene Lockhart to allow the cops to get him. Pepe winds up going after Hedy, leaving the compound, running to the harbor and shouting for her to come back as her ship is about to sail, only she can't hear him because of the ship's horn. Just as Javert doggedly pursued Jean Valjean in *Les Miserables,* Calleia pursues Pepe, and as the boat moves away from the dock, the detective's hand clamps down on the doomed Pepe's shoulder.

That's the basic story. The movie contains some great sixteen millimeter footage of the ferret-like scurryings in the Algiers streets. The nefarious characters who populate the quarter are examined like in a *National Geographic* film—"Negroes from every corner of the African continent! Women of all shapes and sizes willing to please the taste of any man!" It's a great sideshow.

It's Hedy Lamarr who interests me most of all, of course. It was impossible for Pepe not to be swept away once he looked into her perfect face. He was ready for the fall; in fact, he needed it. And that's the point. Pepe had to mark his own fate, to be willing to get caught, to find something or someone worth giving himself over for. It wasn't the sultry Hedy who mattered so much as that it was the right time for it to happen. The only way to avoid disaster is to convince yourself that happiness is what you've got. And then you'll never know whether you're right or wrong. Pepe made it happen, and when he toppled, he was ready. He'd really just gone as far as he could in that place. Hedy played the role of the tethered goat at the tiger trap. It would have taken a lesser man to not take the leap.

The American Friend

1977. Directed by Wim Wenders. Based on Patricia Highsmith's novels *Ripley's Game* and *Ripley Underground*. Starring Bruno Ganz, Dennis Hopper, Sam Fuller, Nicholas Ray, Lisa Kreuger, Gerard Blain.

This movie seems to confuse people. They find it flawed, verbose, prolix, boring. Of all the "homage" films made since the 1940s and '50s meant to evoke *noir*, *The American Friend* succeeds more than most because of the spaces, the sputters, and sudden shifts of energy that allow the characters to achieve veracity.

Bruno Ganz is a picture framer in Hamburg who learns he's going to die within a short time, though he's still a young man with a wife and child. Through a series of circumstances he agrees to murder a mobster for money to leave his family after he's gone. The man he is to kill is in Paris. Dennis Hopper is a wealthy alcoholic American—the Friend of the title—involved in a painting forgery scheme with Nick Ray (who's in New York doing the forgeries; Hopper sells the paintings in Europe). Hopper gets hip to Ganz and their relationship takes over the movie, Hopper doing a bizarre imitation of William S. Burroughs when he helps Ganz out by murdering a guy on a train. As is usual in Highsmith's stories, there is a strong suggestion of homosexual association here. Ganz is driven mad by the whole plot and the runover. Sam Fuller, the director, appears as a porno filmmaker who's also involved in the gangland murders. Hopper lives in a huge, half-empty roundhouse in Hamburg. One of his best scenes takes place in a state of drugged self-absorption one night, snapping photos of himself like masturbating, passing out in a delirious seminightmare.

The real dramatic life of this movie is in the undertow, the way Wenders meanders broodingly, using Ganz as his amanuensis, stroking the viewer with images, making all colors seem brown at their core—the world turning to shit. Startling shots of the Hamburg harbor from the Ganz family's apartment windows don't help alleviate the doomed countenance of the picture. Ganz's wife, Lisa Kreuger, doesn't understand what's happening to her husband. She reacts in that mean, sexy way, with her powerful German jaw and warrior's eyes, straining to involve herself, which she does until the whole thing's played out on a bleak wintry beach.

Wenders allows the mood to become heavy, savage, uncontrollably black/brown. There are gaps designed to involve the viewer, to convey the experience of desperation and madness, depression. A dim world-view, to say the least. Everyone and everything's fraud, like the forged paintings. What kind of future is there for Ganz's kid? The wife probably takes the child and moves to Hawaii after this. I would.

Angels with Dirty Faces

1938. Directed by Michael Curtiz. Starring James Cagney, Humphrey Bogart, The Dead End Kids, Pat O'Brien, and Ann Sheridan.

Billy Halop, Huntz Hall, Gabe Dell, Leo Gorcey, and the others got the name "Dead End Kids" from the 1937 movie *Dead End*, in which they portrayed slum kids on New York's Lower East Side. They went on to make a series of films as The Bowery Boys, a moderately successful run that carried into the 1950s, by which time most of the "boys" were, if not exactly approaching decrepitude, certainly not capable of carrying off successfully the illusion of being gang kids pulling silly adolescent pranks. Hollywood rode the charade too far, and their later movies are just plain junk. However, the early efforts, where they are teamed up with Bogart, Cagney, and Garfield (*They Made Me a Criminal*, 1939), among other leading actors of the day, are terrific. Not least among them is this one, *Angels with Dirty Faces*. It is, in fact, even more than *Dead End*, the quintessential Dead End Kids movie. Most of the credit for this must go to Cagney, who, as the gangster Rocky Sullivan, plays to the hilt the older version of the kids themselves: he's what they'll be in a few years if they continue to live their punk lifestyle. Rocky is released from prison a hardened criminal, and goes back to his old neighborhood—the Lower East Side, of course. The kids don't know who he is when they spot him walking down the street; they figure he's some simple mark and they lift his wallet, then run off. Rocky, however, tracks them to his old lair, a basement hideout, and surprises them as they're counting his money. He sticks an empty hand under his jacket pocket and pretends to point a gun at them. Most of the boys quake and shiver and beg for mercy, but Billy Halop, the leader, sneers and says, "Shut up, rats!" He's the tough guy, the up-and-coming Rocky. Rocky shows them his initials carved into the basement wall, done years before, and they're in awe. It's Rocky Sullivan! So he becomes the kids' idol and mentor. They all want to be just like him. Rocky goes after Bogey, his former partner, to collect what's due him, so the kids get involved in the world of bigtime, real-life hoods.

At the beginning of the movie, however, we see Rocky as a kid, with his young pal Jerry. They're running from the cops and Rocky helps Jerry get away, but he gets caught and sent to reform school. Jerry grows up to be Pat O'Brien, a priest, of course. But he and Rocky are still friends, and they vie for the loyalty of the boys. "Whaddya hear, whaddya say?" is Rocky's familiar greeting. His upper lip's permanently curled. He romances Ann Sheridan, his neighbor and sister of Bobby Jordan, one of the kids. Ann's a good girl—everybody good in this movie is Irish. When Rocky gets nailed for murder and is about to go to the chair, the Catholic church really raises its head and flares its nostrils. It's not enough that Rocky allows Father Jerry to talk him out of dying in a shootout with the cops, but instead of walking to the electric chair and taking his jolt like the tough guy he is (Cagney does manage to spit in a guard's face just prior to the execution), Jerry convinces him to act scared in order to turn the kids away from him, to dissuade them from living like him, to ennoble himself though it'll look like he went to the chair a frightened rat. It's a hell of a lot to ask, Jerry admits, but the Lord will understand. Rocky tells Jerry to stuff it, but at the last minute he breaks down and kicks and screams. "I don't wanna die!" he yells. "I don't wanna die!" And the Good Father closes his eyes and prays for the deliverance of Rocky's soul. Rocky's really a good kid underneath all the bravado.

This ending stinks. The kids can't believe it the next morning reading the newspaper headline ROCKY DIES YELLOW. Just like the crime reporters at the execution were shocked by Rocky's cave-in. "I told you he wasn't so tough," one of 'em says to another. The kids are horrified, like baseball fans finding out that Joe DiMaggio or another hero took bribes, threw games, was queer. And Father Jerry comes to see the boys, huddled in their collective sadness, shock, and disappointment in the basement clubhouse. Sure, Father Jerry knows about the place: those are his initials carved in the wall right next to Rocky Sullivan's. The boys are his, a gift from Rocky. Sentimental glop. But the movie's full of great lines, lots of action, Bogey and Cagney at their snide, stinging best. The world-as-a-simpler-place category. Raw, dumb America before World War Two. You can feel this movie's stupid joy from start to finish.

The Asphalt Jungle

1950. Directed by John Huston. Based on the novel by W. R. Burnett. Starring Sterling Hayden, Sam Jaffe, Louis Calhern, Jean Hagen, Marilyn Monroe, Barry Kelley, Marc Lawrence, and James Whitmore.

Considered classic *noir*, *The Asphalt Jungle* does not disappoint on repeated viewing. Though Huston's movies have never had the edge, the unpredictability of Nicholas Ray's, Huston was able to consolidate the borrowed effects of B-movie innovators, such as Edgar Ulmer and Jacques Tourneur, and utilize them in such a smooth way that they seem almost original. Huston was a master at integrating seemingly disparate styles and effects to create a coherent whole, delicately textured and free of mistakes. *Jungle* reflects two shades: dark and darker. Huston proved, in movies like this and *Treasure of the Sierra Madre* (1948), and later in *Night of the Iguana* (1964), that he could create atmosphere not so dependent on clever dialogue as in *The Maltese Falcon* (1941), *Across the Pacific* (1942), or *Key Largo* (1948).

Harold Rossen's photography follows the RKO mold of severe half-face close-ups of Sterling Hayden and Jean Hagen—the rawboned country boy Hayden is highlighted like Walker Evans's Depression-era photographs—giving a stark reality to the movement; and Louis Calhern's suave weakling, with his elegant mustache, especially in the kissing scene with the nymphet Marilyn Monroe. Huston knew how to handle his cargo here, how to maneuver them in such a way that shadows inform flesh, filter feelings through lips, eyes, bodies. An ingenious robbery caper is planned by ex-con Doc Riedenschneider, played with appropriate gentility and vulnerability by Sam Jaffe, and he hooks up with crooked lawyer Calhern to back him financially; the robbery team includes an expert safecracker (Anthony Caruso), and Sterling Hayden as the "hooligan," the strongarm guy, and James Whitmore as the getaway driver. The robbers are on the level but Calhern's not, and a bunch of things go wrong, unforeseen difficulties that ultimately queer the entire operation and result in everyone's death or capture. There is a certain amount of moralizing on the part of the police chief (John McIntire), and even a crooked cop is exposed. But the charm of this film is its relentless domino action, the clack of one piece falling against the next until the entire row collapses.

Each character has real individuality, a personality absolutely distinct from the next person, and each is fascinating to watch.

Jaffe is the mastermind with a weakness for young girls. There's a great scene toward the end in a roadhouse, where he gives a bunch of nickels to a teenaged girl (Helene Stanley) so that she can play the jukebox and he can watch her dance, which she does as sexily and prettily as the little old German Jew ex-con could ever imagine; he gets his money's worth, but he also gets caught and is bemused by the circumstances, his flaw. Calhern almost succeeds in stealing the movie, playing softly off the brutish violence displayed by the thug cops and avaricious hoods. The scene where his luscious mistress Monroe pulls away as she kisses him, not really giving him the goods and he too genteel/thankful to press for more, is exquisite. Hayden is the noble one, the hardcase, loyal Kentuckian with a troubled relationship with a girl; and Jean Hagen as "Doll," is an equally loyal type who ends up clinging to her man savagely, as perfect contrast to Monroe/Calhern. Whitmore's also a standup guy, a good friend to Hayden. But nobody can gain in this universe: everything turns up empty, a hustle on both sides of the law, which itself is a scam. The word "criminal" carries a convoluted definition; the streets are filled with spiders and their webs enfold the earth. There's no way out, only memory and money— pure pieces of the puzzle.

Autumn Leaves

1956. Directed by Robert Aldrich. Starring Joan Crawford, Cliff Robertson, Vera Miles.

Other than *Mildred Pierce*, this is the Joan Crawford film most generous to Joan, the one that places her as the object of sympathy. Her looks are hard but in this case it's understandable: she's on the verge of becoming an old maid, a certain spinster, keeping mostly to herself, typing manuscripts, and living in a little apartment in a sidecourt in L.A. She has a friendly, too-yappy older neighbor, the landlady, her only pal. Joan's lonely, and when she accidentally meets a young, decent-looking fellow, played by Cliff Robertson, she's intrigued. His crooked smile, self-deprecating manner, brash-but-gentle, goodnatured behavior disarms her, charms her. The problem, to her, is that he's younger than she is by a few years. Joan's bothered by this, it doesn't sit right with her. Reluctantly she drifts into the affair. Cliff makes her feel good, cajoles her out of her conservative, frightened, mousey ways, *kisses* her in public and makes her feel like a woman, a real woman, like she's never felt before. She's giddy, wild with the smell of love and she's not sure what to do about it.

But of course there's a catch. Cliff moves in with her, they marry, and all seems well. Joan's neighbor-friend is happy to see her so happy. Cliff seems nice enough, a pleasant, slightly cocky young man. Then things begin to go wrong. He's nuts. He doesn't have a job anymore. Joan comes unglued. He gets violent. She doesn't know what to do now, how to get rid of him, how to regain the universe as she knew it. This is the price of taking a chance, she thinks, her worst nightmare.

My mother had a husband like this. A handsome, charming Irishman who seemed fine and then one day just wouldn't get out of bed. He lay there, catatonic, not moving. Turned out he had a metal plate in his head, he'd been injured in the war. Finally she had to get him moved to the Veterans hospital where they told her he'd never be completely well. He'd work for a while, make good money as a salesman and then go off-center for several months. They were married for six months, and my mother got an annulment. Once, after that Bartelbylike attack at our house, I met him with my mom at a park and he looked ragged, worn, unshaven, and scary. His normally blue-green eyes were dark gray; they'd given him drugs in the hospital, maybe primitive electro-shock treatments, I don't know. He wanted to come back, to live with us again but my mother refused. I was upset because I liked him so much; he was always good to me and a fine athlete who played with me a lot. I missed him. But later I understood my mother's decision. He'd never told her about his disability, his spells; he couldn't drive a car, he told her, because of bad vision, not because he was subject to these periodic freakouts without warning. He'd misled her and she was sympathetic but angry, also confused and sad. Some years later, when I was about thirteen, I spotted him walking down the street in front of a big hotel. He was wearing a long blue overcoat, he needed a shave, he fixed his eyes straight ahead of him and walked fast, seemingly purposefully, not noticing others around him on the sidewalk. I wanted to say something, to stop him, but he looked unstoppable, unapproachable, mad.

My mother's favorite song, other than *La Vie en Rose*, was *Autumn Leaves*, and she used to play the piano and sing it when I was a kid. It's the theme song of this movie, a sad song for a sad story.

Badlands

1973. Directed by Terrence Malick. Screenplay by Terrence Malick. Starring Martin Sheen, Sissy Spacek, Warren Oates.

Based on the Charles Starkweather-Caril Fugate murder spree of the mid-1950s, *Badlands* was Malick's first directorial effort—he'd written the Paul Newman/Lee Marvin movie, *Pocket Money*, among others, before this. It's narrated by Sissy, a 15-year-old semimoron in a small Dakota town, who gets swept away by the older Sheen, a garbageman with fancy cowboy boots. They tear up the upper west for a few weeks, killing her father—played by Warren Oates, a sign-painter—first, then whoever gets in the way. Daddy doesn't want this strange, goodlooking sociopath (the James Dean lookalike thing is played up heavily), Sheen, to have anything to do with the skinny, freckle-faced teenaged kid. Sheen attempts to reason with Oates, but then just *has* to shoot him. And we're off and running.

There's great music—Mickey and Sylvia's "Love is Strange" is most apropos—and beautiful photography. It pays to see this one in color, but it works as well in black and white: the great test! It's a marvelously intelligent movie, a rarity. Sheen hijacks a big old Eldorado and they cross the country avoiding roads altogether, tapping fuel from the oil well set-ups owned by private companies. For a time they live like Tarzan and Jane, literally swinging from a tree. Sheen prepares for an invasion, and when it comes, his guerilla preparations pay off: he manages to kill them before they kill him. Sheen insists on being polite to almost everyone, his madness just a wee bit below the surface. He disarms people before wasting them.

Sissy just kind of goes along with it all, excited and thrilled by Sheen's seeming self-assurance, but always scared. She wants to get away but can't figure out how, so she makes the best of it. When he deflowers her she asks, "Is that what everybody gets so excited about?" And he says, "Yeah, that's it." Not the exact words but you get the point—it's a real moment, and their faces are perfect. They dance in the middle of the prairie by kerosene lantern, spend a bizarre spell in the house of some rich people in a small town where Sheen is curious about their mute black maid, as if she—and not he—were from some other planet. After he and Sissy make love by a river he says he's going to keep a big rock he finds by the spot in order to commemorate the event; after a few steps he tosses it away and picks up a smaller one, then tosses it, too. This is an episodic, narratively hungry movie: these two are mad but ingenuous; killing is only part of what they do.

The manhunt becomes gigantic, and Sheen is finally caught, handcuffed, chained, and taken to an Air Force base where all the young National Guard guys strain themselves to get a good look at him: an instant legend, James Dean as mass murderer, the role following *Giant*. On the helicopter at the end, Sheen—whose name is Kit—asks his guard if he thinks the authorities will give him special consideration for having turned himself in. "You're quite an individual, Kit," says the guard (played by John Womack, a buddy of Malick's from Harvard who wrote a great book about Emiliano Zapata). The character of Kit is a lot like the structure of this movie: it meanders but it's meaningful as hell.

The Big Combo

1955. Directed by Joseph H. Lewis. Screenplay by Philip Yordan. Starring Cornel Wilde, Jean Wallace, Brian Donlevy, Richard Conte, Lee Van Cleef, and Earl Holliman.

I have to admit my affection for *The Big Combo* is even greater than it is for Joseph Lewis's earlier *Gun Crazy*. Chiaroscuro is Lewis's domain. There are several remarkable scenes in this movie that belong at the top of the shadow game. The story line is adequate: detective Wilde goes after gangster Conte to shut him down. Trouble within the mob boils over when Donlevy tries to take over for Conte. Conte's moll, Jean Wallace, crosses over to the Wilde side, helping to do Conte in. That's basically it. Lewis liked to use icy blondes the way Hitchcock did. In *Gun Crazy* it was Peggy Cummins; here it's Jean Wallace. But the difference is that Hitchcock's women were classier: Grace Kelly, Kim Novak, Tippi Hedren, etc. Lewis's women are more overtly sex-kittenish, raunchier, like the difference used to be between nudes in *Playboy* as opposed to, say, *Rogue* or *Escapade*. Hitchcock had a bigger budget, too.

Donlevy doublecrosses Conte, tries to get Conte's henchmen, Lee Van Cleef and Earl Holliman, to knock off the boss and follow him; but the dupe fails and Van Cleef and Holliman turn their machine guns on Donlevy. Before Conte tells them to pull the trigger, he walks over to Donlevy and removes his hearing aid; we see the guns fire in the dark, bright flames spitting at the stunned Donlevy, but there's no sound. We become Donlevy, the tentacles of light directed at us and slowed down so that the smoke curls and wraps around the darkness like reticulate pythons. Later in the movie Conte decides to dispose of Van Cleef and Holliman. He hands them a package of what they think is money, food, guns, I forget—they're in a basement hideout—but it's dynamite. When it blows it's in slow motion again, the white piles of flame and smoke slithering over and around each other, another exquisite maze of deathclouds.

Darkness disguises cheap sets—witness even the recent *Blade Runner*—but it takes a visual artist to make the black work, to infect it with just enough light so that anything other than dark seems wrong, uncomfortable, unnatural. Nocturnal contact is different from that of daylight: sex and danger come to the surface much more readily, they inform the frame, the background fills up and comes closer, threatening to over-whelm, to overcome any puny attempt to hold it back. Lewis managed to drain anything unnecessary from this image, to hold it up in dim matchlight for an instant, then snuff it out.

The Big Heat

1953. Directed by Fritz Lang. Based on the novel by William P. McGivern. Starring Glenn Ford, Gloria Grahame, Lee Marvin, Jocelyn Brando, Alexander Scourby, Jeanette Nolan, Carolyn Jones, and Dorothy Green.

Glenn Ford as Detective Sergeant Dave Bannion is really Cru-sader Rabbit as he goes up against crooked cops, city politicians, and big time gangsters and manages to bring "the big heat" down on them all. Along the way he sacrifices the lives of his wife and three other women, at least two of whom he considers no good anyway, and jeopardizes the safety of his daughter, in order to set things straight. In this pursuit of justice he becomes a robotic, maniacal individual, incapable of rest until the bad guys are dead or in custody. *The Big Heat* would be a perfect vehicle for Chuck Norris, and in fact bears no small relation to Norris's *Code of Silence*, his best picture to date.

Ford is investigating the suicide of another cop and is told to lay off by his superiors. The dead cop left a letter implicating crime boss Mike Lagana (Alex Scourby) and his widow is using it to blackmail Lagana. The suicide's mistress is killed, and when Ford doesn't back off, so is Ford's wife. When Ford faces up to his own boss about a tie-in to Lagana, Ford is kicked off the force. Undaunted, Ford hides his daughter so the thugs can't get to her, and goes after Lagana even harder. He tracks down one of Lagana's gunmen, Vince Stone, played to the ruthless end by snarling Lee Marvin, and tries to convince Marvin's moll, Gloria Grahame, to talk to him. She refuses to cooperate but when Marvin sees her with Ford he thinks she's spilling and he throws a cup of scalding coffee in her face, disfiguring her; of course this turns her to Ford.

Gloria Grahame becomes the focus of the movie, the most compelling figure in the entire mess. She's now the whore/saint, bent to wreak vengeance on the miserable Marvin and root out the whole stinking heap. Grahame's sharp-angled face is savage enough to begin with, but after she's burned by the coffee she becomes a kind of she-creature, an untouchable sex bomb. Ford is a machine, and something of a dunderhead besides, so Grahame makes more sense as a *person.* She squeals without compunction now to them about how Lagana and Marvin committed the murders, and hips Ford to the co-opting of the cop commissioner. Grahame gets back at Marvin directly, splattering *his* face with hot coffee, but getting shot in the process. She dies with her ugly side hidden in her fur coat, sleeping with her relaxed, angelic, smooth profile face up to Ford. Ford cracks the crime ring and gets his job back.

McGivern gave the story a perfect cop-opera ending, when he wrote: "Now he was starting over, not with hatred but only sadness. That wasn't too bad, he thought." It's the first *rational* thought Dave Bannion's had so far, but it's still pathetic. Fritz Lang seized on the brute-cop/brute-criminal state of mind to make this movie a *tour de force* of insensitive behavior. That's why Gloria Grahame comes out looking like Mary Magdalene, a slender cut above all the other sick fools caught in the bad light. "Anyone who holds a frying pan owns death," wrote William Burroughs, a perfect epigram for this one.

The Big Steal

1949. Directed by Don Siegel. Starring Robert Mitchum, Jane Greer, William Bendix, Patric Knowles, and Ramon Navarro.

One of Don Siegel's first feature films, *The Big Steal* is nowhere near as complicated as Mitchum and Greer's effort of two years earlier, *Out of the Past.* It's a highly successful chase picture, with plenty of zippy dialogue made livelier than usual by the dynamic between the two leads. Mitchum beats it down to Vera Cruz to recover a stolen Army payroll from Patric Knowles. Mitchum himself is pursued by Bill Bendix, his army superior, a captain, who thinks Mitchum was in cahoots with Knowles and is meeting up with him to split the loot. Mitchum figures he'd better locate Knowles first and hand over the money personally to Bendix or nobody will ever believe he wasn't in on it. Greer is also in pursuit of Knowles because he hustled her for a couple of grand; Mitchum's after three hundred thousand.

Bendix attacks Mitchum in his ship's stateroom just prior to debarkation, but Bob manages to knock Bendix out. He bumps into Greer on the dock and they have a humorous, innuendo-filled conversation about a parrot Mitchum buys from a vendor. They don't know one another. Greer locates Knowles first, but he smooth-talks his way around her, and by the time Mitchum shows up, she's in the shower and Knowles has split. They hook up after relating their stories to each other and take off after Knowles, who's headed inland with the money to a small town. Bendix comes after them, so it's like the Indy 500 down Mexico's Route 66. The automobiles careen around precipitous corners like Evel Knievel, narrowly avoiding donkeys, carts, kids, sheep, cows. Bendix shoots at them as he drives, cracking their rearview mirror, but Mitchum manages to evade him. He takes a side road under construction and Greer convinces the road workers that the bad guy chasing them is her evil father who's trying to force her to marry an ugly old man, not the handsome young Mitchum with whom she's in love. The road gang get them on their way and blocks Bendix, allowing Mitchum and Greer to get to the town ahead of him. There they connect with the local captain of police who has already got an eye on Knowles. Mitchum fills the cops in on the deal and follows Knowles to the fence's hideout over a rough road in the mountains. The weaselly fence has three thugs on guard but Mitchum kills one, wounds another, and gets through to the house where he confronts Knowles. The fence has offered Knowles $150,000 in unmarked bills for the stolen $300,000, pleading difficulty in unloading the hot cash. Soon after Mitchum and Greer stumble in, Bendix crashes the scene: it turns out *he's* the one in league with Knowles, and Knowles is working for him. He doles out a share to Knowles and then shoots him in the back as he starts to leave with it. Mitchum starts a ruckus and the town cops arrive and everything gets straightened out in a hurry. Mitchum recovers the payroll and gets Greer to boot.

The plot is simple but Siegel makes it lively as hell, with wild cutting during the chase scenes. It's easy to pick out the sequences shot exclusively in the studio; they're hokey but topsy-turvy and it's fun to watch Mitchum and Greer goose each other like Bogart and Bacall. Short, sweet, and not too deep.

Blood on the Moon

1948. Directed by Robert Wise. Starring Robert Mitchum, Robert Preston, Barbara BelGeddes, Phyllis Thaxter, Tom Tully, Walter Brennan, and Frank Faylen.

This is the truest western *noir* ever made, straight out of the RKO corral. Robert Wise was a graduate of the Val Lewton School of Shadows and Camera Murk (*The Body Snatcher, Curse of the Cat People,* etc.), and *Blood on the Moon* moves through the same territory as *The Leopard Man* and *Cat People.*

Mitchum plays Jim Gary, a would-be cattle rancher who's lost his herd and goes to work for his old pal Robert Preston. Preston is trying to manipulate a group of homesteaders, featuring Walter Brennan, against a cattleman, Tom Tully, in a struggle over land. What the homesteaders don't know is that Preston's cooked up a deal on the side with the Indian Bureau man, Frank Faylen (who went on to play Dobie's dad in the TV series "The Many Loves of Dobie Gillis"), wherein the two of them stand to cash in to everyone else's disfavor. Preston's a conniving snake, romancing rancher Tully's older daughter, Phyllis Thaxter, in order to get information out of her concerning a cattle drive. He hires a couple of thugs to ride with the homesteaders, and with the outfit bolstered by his buddy Mitchum, the only guy he knows who's as tough as himself, there seems no way Tully can survive.

The real romance, though, is between Bel Geddes, the younger, feistier, cute-not-pretty, Annie Oakley-like daughter of Tully's, and Big Old Lazy-Eyed Hunk-o'-Man Mitchum. Mitch cuts through Tully's land on his way to join up with Preston, not knowing yet what he's riding into, and stumbles across wildcat Bel Geddes, defender of her father's domain and integrity. So they get off on two wrong feet but of course are mightily attracted to one another and we know where this game is headed. It's the perfect playoff for the deceitful Preston and his use of Thaxter, who is made to betray her own father for The Music Man.

Everything in the movie is dark, cloudy—even the scenes in daylight on a snowy mountain where Mitchum kidnaps Faylen after Mitchum turns on Preston and sides with Tully. There never seems to be more than two hours of available light in a day here. It pre-dates *McCabe and Mrs. Miller*, Robert Altman's moody, long-suffering neo-western by a quarter of a century. The only later western to come close to Wise's in terms of feel and look is Stan Dragoti's *Dirty Little Billy* (1972), with Michael J. Pollard as Billy The Kid in one of the slimiest, filthiest, muddiest movies of all time—a real little masterpiece too-little known, another *noir* Night of Nausea (Look out the ghost of J.-P. Sartre!).

Walter Brennan, who looked like he was sixty when he was in his early twenties, plays a pivotal role in *Blood*, coming back to assist Mitchum after first running out when his son is killed by one of Tully's men during a stampede instigated by Preston. Brennan plays his usual crotchety, Wicked Witch of The West/Rumplestiltskin character—the stoic with a heart, though, in this one. Eight years before, he'd been Judge Roy Bean in William Wyler's *The Westerner*, an unredeemed, nasty son of a bitch; but here he comes through for Mitchum and Bel Geddes against Preston's hoods after Mitchum is stabbed in the stomach. Bel Geddes has a pudgy but pert nose—she's the head side of the coin on which Peggy Cummins (*Gun Crazy*, 1949) is the tail; kid sister-tough but just enough of a sex kitten to claw her way up Mount Mitchum.

A dark, cranky, realistic, serious western with enough moonlight and blood on the trail for anyone this side of *Dragoon Wells Massacre* (1957).

The Blue Dahlia

1946. Directed by George Marshall. Screenplay by Raymond Chandler. Starring Alan Ladd, Veronica Lake, William Bendix, Howard da Silva, Doris Dowling, Hugh Beaumont, Howard Freeman, and Will Wright.

The key element of this film is Alan Ladd's post-World War Two malaise, his disillusionment on his return from the battlefield to Los Angeles, where he discovers his wife living a dissolute lifestyle following the death of their only child. Helen (Doris Dowling) has been running around with a nightclub owner, Eddie Harwood (Howard da Silva), who is married to Veronica Lake. Ladd meets up by accident with Lake, who offers him a ride on a rainy night. Ladd is disgusted by everyone and everything; the whole world is cockeyed since the war and he's not sure where he fits into it, if anywhere. He's ready to blow off the few friends he has left, but he's tied to Buzz (William Bendix), his war buddy who's plagued by dizzy spells, amnesia, and blackouts due to a war injury, and George (Hugh Beaumont), the most levelheaded of the bunch.

Dad Newell (played by Will Wright, who later opened a superb ice cream parlor in Hollywood) is a hotel dick who tries to blackmail Ladd's wife over her affair with Eddie. When Helen is murdered the cops put out an APB for Ladd, figuring he's the culprit, having axed his wife when he discovered her infidelities. Ladd, however, thinks it may have been his pal Buzz who killed her during one of his seizures. Buzz can't stand loud noises—he screams at people to cut out playing "that monkey music" because it gives him a headache. George and Ladd continually have to calm Buzz down to keep him out of trouble, talking to him soothingly as one would to a crazed pit bull. Buzz is fiercely loyal to them. Ladd bumps into Lake again down the coast at a seaside hotel where they've both gone separately to get away from their troubles—she's estranged from her nightclub owner husband Eddie and Ladd is on the run. He gives Lake a phony name, but she recognizes him from his picture in the newspaper and from radio bulletins. Finally he sees that she's more his type than his dead wife and they develop a tentative, casual relationship based on mutual sympathy. They also look great together: they look alike; they blend well, their soft, blonde, raised-eyebrow laid-back personae translate perfectly in black and white, a relationship born in 1942 in *This Gun for Hire*.

Lake helps Ladd out as he does all he can to find out who really killed his wife, more to discover whether or not Buzz did it than to avenge her death. It turns out that Dad did it, frustrated over his failed attempt; Eddie and Ladd are cleared and Lake and Ladd are free to try and work out a legitimate partnership. Chandler's original idea was to make the shellshocked Buzz responsible for killing Ladd's wife, but the Navy objected and he was forced to pin it on Dad Newell, a rather unlikely candidate. It's more likely Ladd himself would have done it. But this is good postwar rainy night action, with Ladd and Lake like a more intelligent, decent Peggy Cummins and John Dall of *Gun Crazy*. Lake's hair is tied back from her face at the request of the War Department because too many women were copying her hair-over-the-right-eye style and it was getting in the way of their factory work, even causing accidents. She was perfect for Ladd, especially since she was one of the very few leading ladies shorter than he was.

Bob Le Flambeur

1955. Directed by Jean-Pierre Melville. Starring Roger Duchesne, Isabelle Corey, and Daniel Cauchy.

In English, *Bob The Gambler*. According to Melville, this is his first original script, and he modeled it after John Huston's *The Asphalt Jungle*. What turned out is a lighthearted but rather beautiful as well as suspenseful film, somewhat underrated in the grand scheme of French cinema. It's actually kind of a Gallic beatnik movie, set as it is in Paris in the 1950s. Bob, played by Roger Duchesne, is a professional gambler who's done some hard time. He rolls around the city in a big Buick (I think) convertible, an American dragon, and cuts quite an impressive figure with his high wavy pompadour, smooth looks, and casual manner. He spots a girl on the street, a kind of lost soul, and lets her stay at his place—a great *atelier*-like flat straight out of *La Bohème*.

Director Melville says that he spotted Isabelle Corey, who plays the girl, walking in the Place de Madeleine in Paris, and approached her. Apparently she was only fifteen at the time and was living on her own. Well, she was one of the most mature looking fifteen year olds I've ever seen, a living doll with a proto-Nastassia Kinski face and a full but sleek figure. Nothing goes on between Bob and this girl in a romantic way; she eventually takes up with a pal of his, Pablo (played by Daniel Cauchy). Bob is trying to stay clean but he gets roped into pulling off a casino heist at Deauville. The girl complicates things, of course, and the robbery fails, but Bob, who, despite his profession, is well thought of by the cops because he's such a gentleman, gets off. The girl goes her own way, headed for trouble.

The pull of this movie is the ambiance, the casual touch administered by Bob's demeanor, and the girl's lazy approach to life—she's highly aware of her power over men, and the envy and hatred she arouses in older women. She's a slut, a Jim Thompson female, a hell of a woman. The laidback jazz score suits her perfectly, and Duchesne's suave, self-assured but not arrogant Bob leavens the heat she injects. Melville's Montmartre underworld is seedy and unsavory but not American-brutal. There's violence but it's all on the surface and often comical, which is appropriate to the story. In his film *Le Samourai* (*The Samurai*), Melville made a serious attempt to profile a hired gun, played by Alain Delon, but it was a fiasco. Despite what certain *noir* aficionados and critics have said, *Samourai* is phony from the tip of Delon's fedora to the toes of his spitshined black shoes. There's one fine metro chase sequence but that's it. Melville made his antihero too self-conscious, so it comes out as a pretentious attempt at American *noir*. Wim Wenders did it much better years later in *The American Friend* because he added confusion and humor.

Bob remains Melville's best effort. It's worth it to see Isabelle Corey at her sauciest, insouciant best. Come and get it, she taunts, and you'll come away emptier than you were before. Bob the gambler's the only smart one: he knows better than to bet the store on a maiden at five furlongs no matter how good she looks.

Body and Soul (See *City for Conquest*)

Body Heat

1981. Directed by Lawrence Kasdan. Starring William Hurt, Kathleen Turner, Richard Crenna, Ted Danson, and Mickey Rourke.

If it weren't for William Hurt's presence in this movie, I doubt seriously that I would bother to write about it. Hurt is one of the finest actors to come along in many years; he's right up there with Robert DeNiro so far as I'm concerned, exhibiting a range not unlike that of a young Alec Guinness. This may seem rather lavish praise for such a young actor, but both Guinness and Hurt are bland, indefinite-looking men; their actual personalities and looks do not invade the characters they portray. They're malleable, unthreatening. Hurt often rises above the material (viz. *Kiss of the Spider Woman* and *The Big Chill*), the same way Guinness was always able to put his stamp on a picture. (I can actually imagine Hurt doing as effective a job as Sir Alec did with Gulley Jimson!).

Anyway, *Body Heat* is *noir* enough but not realistic enough. Its main flaw for me is that I can't imagine Hurt's character going all the way down the toilet for Kathleen Turner; she just doesn't grab me enough, I guess. Turner plays a femme fatale who seduces Hurt, a small-town Florida lawyer (a bad one) into helping her murder her husband (Richard Crenna) so that she can collect his fortune and they'll be able to run away together. The trick is that Hurt thinks she's doing it just for him, that she can't inherit Crenna's money. Suffice it to say she pulls a royal number on him, uses him hard, then throws him to the sharks while she takes off forever. The beauty of it is how Hurt is made to feel that he is the aggressor, completely unsuspecting of the possibility he's being set up. Kasdan does a good job there, and he throws in enough rustling palm leaves, clanging wind chimes, and sweaty foreheads to usher in a grand sexual rush. One nice scene has Turner face down naked being banged from behind, Hurt out of the shot, while she gasps "Don't . . . uh . . . uh . . . stop." This is something we didn't see in, say, *White Heat*—Steve Cochran ramming it home to Virginia Mayo. And while we did get it in the remake of *The Postman Always Rings Twice*, with Jessica Lange and Jack Nicholson, somehow it didn't ring completely true; it was too out front. The Turner character is working in this; she's a complete whore, playing Hurt until he'll sacrifice anything for her. In Lange/Nicholson's case it's (supposed to be) real passion we're seeing. For some reason, the con carries more power; and though I had a hard time identifying with Hurt, it was only because Turner wasn't the right girl for me.

There's a wonderful little performance by Mickey Rourke in this as an explosives expert Hurt once defended. Rourke is sharp and funny, wiser than Hurt, and gives him some good advice that Hurt, naturally enough, ignores. Ted Danson plays off Hurt nicely, too, literally dancing his way through the movie as a fellow lawyer. And Crenna, as the husband, plays it small; the interesting thing is that he doesn't appear to be half as bad as Turner makes him out to be. Only someone as pussywhipped as Hurt gets could fall into the trap. She done him wrong but good.

Born to Be Bad

1950. Directed by Nicholas Bay. Starring Joan Fontaine, Joan Leslie, Zachary Scott, Robert Ryan and Mel Ferrer.

This is Joan Fontaine's foxiest role, and a difficult one, akin to Anne Baxter's sweet little terror in *All About Eve*, made the same year. Fontaine plays Kristabel, the poor-flower cousin from Santa Flora, who comes to San Francisco under the sponsorship of her Uncle John, a well-to-do publisher. Kristabel is supposed to attend business college and live with Uncle John's assistant, Donna, played by the beautiful Joan Leslie. Donna's engaged to Zachary Scott (Curtis Carey), a wealthy socialite, and is buddies with Robert Ryan (Nick Bradley), a novelist, and Mel Ferrer, a gay painter who hustles the rich folks. In short order, Kristabel starts an affair with Nick, betrays Donna's kindness by moving in on Curtis, disappoints her Uncle John when she bags business school before she even gets started, and promotes an uneasy alliance with Ferrer, who knows a sharp but subtle climber when he sees one.

Little Miss Innocence insinuates herself into Curtis's confidence, and soon he suspects that Donna's just after him for his money. Kristabel plays it very small when she's around him, The Poor Little Match Girl routine, and he falls for her. Meanwhile, Kristabel is carrying on a torrid sex-beast scene with the writer, whose book is bought by Uncle John's firm. Nick tells Kristabel the good news and asks her to marry him but she shocks him by instead accepting a proposal from Curtis. This weirds out everyone except Ferrer, who knows his portrait of the scandalous lady is going to be worth a bunch someday. Nick takes off for Boston, Donna goes to London, and Kristabel settles into life at the Carey mansion, becoming a manipulative social maven. She still smiles sweetly and glides merrily along, shafting people in the coolest fashion possible, including her aged Aunt Clara, who raised her, exiling her back to Santa Flora after Curtis had made her welcome in San Francisco because she wants no reminders of her humble origin.

Kristabel's got Curtis snowed—he hardly notices that cash kicks off her shoulders like dandruff and that she manages to find a double dozen reasons to avoid making love with him. When Nick comes back to town, though, she streaks to him like a heat-seeking missile. The only trouble is that Nick won't be her "backstreet boy," as he tells her. She wants it both ways, of course, the money and the hungry artist. Her downfall comes when one day she makes a date to see Nick and tells Curtis she's gone off to aid her ailing Aunt Clara in Santa Flora. On her return from the tryst, Uncle John and Curtis confront her with the news that Aunt Clara has died and that they'd been trying to get in touch with her all day. Nick's quits with her, too, because she's refused to get a divorce, and Donna's returned from London to reclaim Curtis. Mel Ferrer is happy, though, because his portrait of Kristabel, as he figured, is now worth a bundle, and he helps her pack up her Caddy convertible, loaded with booty. Kristabel's still smiling, having a bountiful divorce settlement to look forward to.

It's a soap opera, sure, but a crafty one, however overwrought at times. Nick Ray keeps a good balance, with the fiery writer played off against the foppish painter played off against the rich naïf, and decent dame embattled by the amoral schemer. The interesting thing is that despite the picture's title, despite virtually all of the other characters' ultimate view of her, Kristabel cannot even momentarily entertain the notion of "bad" as pertains to herself. The only time she gets disturbed is when things don't tumble according to her master plan. At the end she's immeasurably better off than when she came in and she doesn't really feature what the fuss has been about. I've only met one person in my lifetime who didn't have at least a little bit of Kristabel in them, and I married her.

Born to Kill

1947. Directed by Robert Wise. Based on the novel *Deadlier Than the Male* by James Gunn. Starring Lawrence Tierney, Claire Trevor, Audrey Long, Walter Slezak, Elisha Cook, Jr., Philip Terry, Esther Howard, and Isabel Jewell.

Made the same year as *The Devil Thumbs A Ride, Born to Kill* was a comparatively starstudded production directed by Robert Wise, a veteran of the RKO/Val Lewton stable. Wise had also worked with Orson Welles and knew his way around low-budget horror and suspense productions. Tierney's menacing presence is as volatile here as in *Devil*, but the circumstances are slicker—no more believable, really, but more sophisticated. Again, the big lug is a squinty-eyed killer, a rock-hard devil with women, the big brute fantasy come alive in all of his horrifying glory.

Claire Trevor is her usual fidgety-lipped, almost-glamor girl, in Reno to get a divorce so she can marry her rich San Francisco boyfriend. She's rooming at Mrs. Craft's (played with loud affection by Esther Howard, who practically steals the movie), who must be some kind of former whorehouse madame. Mrs. Craft and her neighbor Isabel Jewell, a decent sort of slut, are great pals. The night before Trevor's departure for Frisco, she goes out to gamble a little, and at the craps table locks eyes with the demon-man, Tierney. Tierney, however, spots his former girlfriend Jewell out with another man. Later that night, Tierney murders both Jewell and her new fella, and gets out of Mrs. Craft's house before the bodies are discovered by Claire Trevor. Trevor decides not to get involved and leaves Reno on the next train south. Tierney's pal, Elisha Cook, Jr., advises Tierney—

whose name is Wild—after Tierney confesses the murders to him—to get out of town fast. So, of course Tierney and Trevor take the train together. He charms her—sort of. She's attracted to him but freaked out, too. He comes on too tough, too strong. He's not a "turnip," like most men, and he comes to see her at her San Francisco home. Tierney takes up with Trevor's foster sister, a sweet young blonde (Audrey Long), and within a few short weeks marries her. Long is a newspaper heiress, and he has his sights set on running the family newspaper. Trevor is insanely jealous, and Tierney is still crazy about her, too.

Then everybody from Reno turns up: Elisha Cook, Mrs. Craft, and the detective Mrs. Craft hires to find out who murdered her friend. Now things really go haywire. Tierney ends up killing his own friend, Cook, because he mistakenly believes Cook is coming on to Trevor; everybody is hustling everybody else and threatening bodily harm or worse: Trevor's fiancé walks out on her; the good sister discovers Tierney and Trevor's mad passion for each other; Tierney murders Trevor and the cops kill him. It's all a jumble of improbable events and hopeless passions. Somehow, Wise managers to mark it all out so that it makes movie sense, but it never really jells. What does work, however, is the tension, the individual scenes of menace, mainly the presence of the maniacal Tierney, who seems to bring out the worst in others.

The camera angles are interesting, too, especially the scene where Tierney is lying on his bed smoking a cigarette and talking on the telephone. As he talks the camera eye, located directly above him, slowly descends: we get caught up in the conversation so that by the time he hangs up the camera eye is right down on his broad, evil face and we don't know quite how it got there. There's no decency at all in Lawrence Tierney's face, the most cruelly handsome visage on film. Unlike Mitchum's face there's no relief in sight, a man incapable of compromise.

Call Northside 777

1948. Directed by Henry Hathaway. Starring James Stewart, Richard Conte, Lee J. Cobb, Kasia Orzazewski, Helen Walker, and E. G. Marshall.

Nice shots of Chicago alleys and porches, wash flapping in the wind. James Stewart is a newspaperman, based on the old Chicago *Times* reporter James P. McGuire, whose articles helped to free Frank Wiecek and Tomek Zaleska, both of whom had been falsely accused and convicted eleven years earlier for murdering a cop in a speakeasy. Cobb is the editor who gets Stewart on the case, and Conte is Wiecek, whose story we follow. In an effort to get her son out of prison, Wiecek's poor old mother is scrubbing floors to save up enough money to offer a reward for information leading to the real killers. Stewart is cynical at first, fights Cobb about doing the feature, but eventually becomes obsessed with the case and convinced of Frank and Tomek's innocence.

The good thing about this story is that the liars don't budge and the consequences of the situation are irreversible. This is no fairytale. Wiecek has a wife and little son when he goes up; he tells the wife to divorce him and start a new life—99 years is too long to wait. She does so, but still wants to help get him out. The woman who identified Frank in the first place obviously lied about it, but even in the face of new evidence to the contrary, she sticks to her story. When Frank finally does get out he can at least see his son on weekends; and because Stewart (called McNeal in the movie) was able to spring him while on assignment, Frank's mother doesn't have to pay him the $5,000 she'd offered in her newspaper ad.

But the most interesting feature of the movie is how, using this semidocumentary style, Chicago is revealed as a hard town—not fancifully or romantically, but in the faces, streets, weather, conversation, attitude. It's a mean city, and was meaner in the 1940s and '50s than it is in the '80s. Citizens respect the fix, influence, and the long arm. Guys like McNeal are bleeding hearts, but the interesting sidelight is the sentimentality inherent in the people. If you can take the battering long enough to convince them you got guts, and if you then prove you didn't deserve the battering in the first place, you're a made man. That's what happened to Frank Wiecek, but he lost eleven years, his marriage, and the chance to see his kid grow up. Mike Ditka, coach of the Chicago Bears, described other teams as being composed of a bunch of guys named Smith; the Bears, he said, are Grabowskis.

The way the reporter is stymied by the cops in his effort to examine police records supposedly open to anyone; the refusal of the primary "witness" to admit her "error" even when confronted by the truth; the newspaper publisher quitting the case when the going gets rough; the terrible grayness that pervades everything about Chicago: all this makes life in the big city seem hardly worth living. It's a battle to survive anywhere, but it can be tougher in Chicago, much tougher. That's what this movie's about.

Cape Fear

1962. Directed by J. Lee Thompson. Based on the novel *The Executioners* by John D. MacDonald. Starring Robert Mitchum, Gregory Peck, Polly Bergen, Martin Balsam, Telly Savalas, and Lori Martin.

Mitchum is a giant of evil in this movie; a slithery, completely corrupt, malevolent force. Along with his role as the crazed preacher in *Night of the Hunter,* this is arguably his finest performance. The supporting cast complements Mitchum admirably, but if anyone ever had any doubts about his ability to act, this film dispelled them.

A vicious ex-con, Mitchum shows up in the small North Carolina town where Peck is the chief prosecuting attorney. It was Peck who put Mitchum away for eight years for a hideous sex crime and Mitchum has used that time well, plotting his revenge on Peck. A low-rent redneck, Mitchum's take on women is less than charitable. He decides to get back at Peck through Peck's wife and daughter. Along the way he kills the family's dog, savagely beats a girl he picks up in a bar, terrorizes Peck's daughter (she's about thirteen) after school one day, and fails to crack under the brutal bum's rush dished out to him by the local police (Balsam and Savalas). Mitchum swaggers and leers and makes lewd comments to waitresses, establishing him as a number one criminally insane bad boy. He's up front to Peck about his motives and makes Peck squirm. All of this drives Peck to send his family out of town to stay on a houseboat the family keeps on the Cape Fear river. He guesses right, belatedly, that Mitchum will come after them there, and we get the inevitable final fight to the death.

All of the above is predictable enough: we get the set-up right away. The art is in the details, the gradual build-up of fear, the play on the title. Polly Bergen and Lori Martin are wide-eyed and delectably vulnerable as the wife and daughter; Peck is magisterial and vain-stupid but brave; Balsam is careful and decent as the Police Chief pal of Peck's. But this is Mitchum's meat. He's the angel of death-with-pain, put on earth to give men pause. When he describes to Peck how he got back at his ex-wife after he got out of prison, kidnapping her from her new husband and holding her captive in a motel room for days, raping and torturing her, and finally throwing her naked and filled with whiskey onto the road, we hear The Truth; it's a swift lesson in the validity of Bad. Mitchum is The Other and there's no ignoring him. The only way to stop this sonofabitch is with a bullet in the brainpan.

Cape Fear is heavy on Spanish moss and sick behavior, a classic demonstration of the differences between rich and poor; to say nothing of the typical good ol' Southern boy's view of women. Unfortunately, there aren't many of 'em have very much good to say. You won't forget this movie, especially if you're a Yankee Jew.

Cat People (See *I Walked with a Zombie*)

Champion (See *City for Conquest*)

Charley Varrick

1973. Directed by Don Siegel. Based on the novel *The Looters* by John Reese. Starring Walter Matthau, Joe Don Baker, Felicia Farr, and Sheree North.

One of the least-sung, rarely seen chase movies of fairly recent vintage, *Charley Varrick* is probably Don Siegel's best effort since the original *Invasion of the Body Snatchers*. Matthau is lanky and lugubrious as Charley Varrick, a small-time, small-town bank robber who lives in a trailer and likes to keep out of the way. Matthau brings a low-key, commonsense presence—reminiscent of his role as the sheriff in *Lonely are the Brave*—into what is otherwise an hysterical atmosphere. It's a fascinating technique because this is difficult to bring off without seeming phony or pretentious. Matthau is a master at it: he had it down early in his career as the gangster in *King Creole* with Elvis, lending that movie a subtlety and credibility it might not have had otherwise.

Varrick knocks over an independent, federally unconnected New Mexico bank, expecting to take in under a hundred thousand dollars—certainly no large haul. What he couldn't know in advance was that the Mafia used the bank as a money laundering drop and Varrick gets away with a couple of million. Thrilled and horrified both, Matthau disposes of his hillbilly kid partner and takes off; he knows the mob will be on his tail *toute de suite.*

What ensues—The Chase—is made especially horrifying due to the unusual persona of the hit-and-recovery man, played by Joe Don Baker. Baker's killer is smart, mean, and seemingly indestructible, a flesh and blood Terminator not at all like a comic book muscleman. (He smokes a pipe!) We see him repossess a Cadillac from a big tough black guy in front of the guy's wife/girlfriend, leaving the man writhing in agony. When Baker needs a headquarters to work from while he pursues Charley Varrick, he sets up in a mob-run whorehouse. One of the prostitutes comes on to him and he looks at her as if she were slime. "Get the hell away from me, you stupid cretin," he tells her, or words to that effect. Baker is a relentless, amoral killing machine; he brings Real Terror to the screen. Every day he's around is Friday the 13th.

Varrick, however, is a crafty, coyotelike character who's been dodging bullets of one kind or another all his life. A former barnstorming trick pilot, he manages to head off the Mafia moose at the final pass in a unique car–small plane duel worthy of comparison to Manolete fighting a Miura bull. This movie is dusty and low-rent, a late 20th-century western with no generous souls. We admire Varrick for his cleverness, his ability to slide by, but his horizon is a colorless L.A., a low-profile one-eye-over-the-shoulder existence. Guys like him drive past you on the freeway every day.

Chinatown

1974. Directed by Roman Polanski. Starring Jack Nicholson, Faye Dunaway, John Huston, Perry Lopez, John Hillerman, Darrell Zwerling, Diane Ladd, Burt Young, and Roman Polanski.

Not pleasant. This vision, as scripted by Robert Towne and interpreted by Roman Polanski, of Los Angeles in 1937, is as hellish as Phenix City, Alabama in 1955, or Dashiell Hammett's Poisonville. It's a terrifying film, full of corrupt behavior, including greed of virtually every type. Jack Nicholson, as a private investigator specializing in divorce work, gets tricked into a case involving diversion of valley water during a drought in order to make the land available for development; rape, murder, and incest; and, in a lesser fashion, political influence peddling.

Polanski twisted the ending out of Towne's hands and made the movie even darker than intended; and he inserted a scene in which he slices up Jack Nicholson's nose with a large knife. The landscape is hot, dusty, dry; the colors are sere, yellow; the light bleached, smeary.

John Huston's presence in the movie, as the arch-villain Noah Cross, links it to earlier *noir*, including, most notably, his own *The Asphalt Jungle*, In *Jungle*, which is something of a compilation of various black and white *noir* styles, the land-scape is hard and corruption is limited to the professional bad guys and the odd bad cop, whereas in *Chinatown* the sleaze covers everyone; the one decent person, the water commissioner and husband of Faye Dunaway, Noah Cross's daughter, is murdered. The word "Chinatown" signifies more than a section of the city: it's a state of mind, of fear, a place where things once went wrong for Nicholson when he was a policeman and now represents a kind of Neighborhood of Doom. That's a great touch, and Polanski takes it a giant step beyond by injecting his own peculiar, bizarre brand of terror.

So much has been written about this film that it seems re-dundant to carry on about it now. It works, it's frightening; the world is a goddamn disgusting place as exhibited here. Burt Young provides fine comic relief; Faye Dunaway sheds her mysterious veneer like a snake losing its skin; Jack Nicholson is in every scene and plays the fool to a T; John Huston is as menacingly ugly as a human being can possibly be. As Huston says to Nicholson in the movie, at any one moment anyone is capable of doing anything. No excuses, just laying it out for real. This is *film noir outré*, outside the usual boundary of darkness. It makes living somewhere else, even in Cedar Rapids, Iowa, say, look pretty good.

City for Conquest

1940. Directed by Anatole Litvak. Starring James Cagney, Arthur Kennedy, Ann Sheridan, Frank McHugh, Elia Kazan, and Anthony Quinn.

Body and Soul

1947. Directed by Robert Rossen. Starring John Garfield, Lili Palmer, William Conrad, Canada Lee, Hazel Brooks, and Joseph Pevney.

Champion

1949. Directed by Mark Robson. Starring Kirk Douglas, Marilyn Maxwell, Lola Albright, Arthur Kennedy, and Ruth Roman.

The Set-Up

1949. Directed by Robert Wise. Starring Robert Ryan and Audrey Totter.

Somebody Up There Likes Me

1956. Directed by Robert Wise. Starring Paul Newman, Pier Angeli, Everett Sloan, Sal Mineo, and Eileen Heckart.

Raging Bull

1983. Directed by Martin Scorsese. Starring Robert DeNiro, Cathy Moriarty, Joe Pesci, and Theresa Saldana.

Each of these is, in its own way, a superb, realistic evocation of the sweet science and what it does to you. *City for Conquest* is notable primarily for Cagney's skill as a boxer, borrowing on his dancer's moves. Professional fighters have often praised Cagney for his ring savvy, and certainly of all of the above movies he was the one who most *looked* like he belonged between the ropes. (Robert Ryan, however, was an amateur boxer in his youth.) *City*'s tearjerker plot has Cagney going blind from resin rubbed into his eyes by a rival, his brother Kennedy going on to become a great composer while Jimmy is relegated to being a newsstand vendor. Ann Sheridan, the good girl, gets seduced and abandoned by Anthony Quinn as a greaseball (Jewish?) ballroom hoofer named Murray Burns. Plenty of schmaltz and typical 1930s-style New York City melodrama, but the fight scenes are fine because of Cagney's elegant footwork and quick hands. A good lightweight, just like the movie.

Body and Soul reaches further, as does *The Set-Up*, with the protagonists triumphing over greedy gamblers and hoods and deciding not to throw a fight. James Wong Howe's hand-held camera in *Body and Soul* was able to zero in even more dramatically than usual because he wore roller skates in the ring while he filmed. John Garfield plays a boxer who watches everybody fall around him, his mother, his best friend, his girl, while he climbs to the top; at the last, of course, he throws over the devil and straightens up and flies right. Ryan, in *The Set-Up*, is an old fighter at the end of the line, whose manager agrees for him to take a dive and doesn't even bother to tell Ryan, so certain is he that Ryan will lose anyway. When Ryan is on the verge of winning and is told that he's got to dump, he refuses, even though it means he'll have to pay for it later by taking a vicious beating by the hoods.

These are victory-of-the-human-spirit stories, straight out of the '30s, stars-in-the-eyes stuff. But both Garfield and Ryan were well-known Liberals and so these movies are political statements by Directors Rossen and Wise, especially significant as America headed hard into the McCarthy Era. The fight scenes are all well-done and Ryan firmly established himself as a great *noir* actor capable of evincing a troubled countenance combined with keen intelligence.

Champion was the most vicious fight film until *Raging Bull*. Kirk Douglas scraps his way from the bottom to the top, spurred on by a vision of possessing blonde sexpot Marilyn Maxwell, whom he first encounters when he's on the road, a bum in a leather jacket, and can't get her to give him the time of day. He blasts his way out of obscurity by screwing over all of the decent folks and finally gets Maxwell, but he discovers he's just a pawn in the mobsters' game and as helpless as ever. The fight scenes are savage, cruel, and belie A. J. Liebling's label. It's interesting to note that both Mark Robson, who directed *Champion*, and Robert Wise, who directed both *The Set-Up* and *Somebody Up There Likes Me*, were graduates of the RKO/Val Lewton/Jacques Tourneur horror group; they were experts in the use of chiaroscuro and knew how to make a scary picture. That ability is most notably evident in *Champion* and *Set-Up* in the disfigured facial closeups, and in *Somebody* when Newman as Rocky Graziano, briefly the middle-weight champion of the world, whines and spits and grimaces in pain; graphic physical rather than psychological suffering exhibited in Lewton thrillers like *The Body Snatcher* (Wise) or *The Seventh Victim* (Robson).

Graziano's story is a superficial forerunner to Scorsese's *Raging Bull*, the painful portrait of another New York fighter, Jake LaMotta. DeNiro's performance is quite incredible, especially when he plays LaMotta several years into his retirement as a fat slob—he gained sixty pounds in order to look the part. Most of the fight scenes are in slow motion, with the sound slowed down, too, which makes the bone-crunching blows even more horrifying. When I first saw the boxers' faces pushed out of shape in slo-mo I was immediately reminded of that famous photograph of Jersey Joe Walcott sustaining a punch from Rocky Marciano, where his cheek, nose—one entire side of his head—looks like a sideways *W*, with one eye practically popped out of its socket. Scorsese chose to film in black and white, using everything Wise, Robson, and Rossen established and adding his own particular genius to create a masterwork. Cathy Moriarty and Joe Pesci, as LaMotta's wife and brother, are unforgettable victims of the pressures attendant to the life of a professional fighter. There's no way they can avoid getting hit, too. And DeNiro really does take elements of his forerunners—Ryan, Garfield, Cagney, Newman—and incorporates them into his LaMotta persona. *Bull* is somehow stark but elegiac, elegant but brutal. Again the fix is in, the gamblers rule and have their way. The whole business is ugly, and everyone involved gets uglier and covered with blood, spit, and sleaze. Robson's 1956 film, *The Harder They Fall*, a fight movie with Humphrey Bogart as a boxing writer turned fight promoter tied into a gambling syndicate, is a straightforward indictment of the profession, showing how elaborate and despicable the setup can be. LaMotta was a great fighter—his six matches with Sugar Ray Robinson are unequaled, classic contests—and Graziano less so, but both were dupes the same as the palookas portrayed by Garfield, Ryan, and Douglas, as exploited as the glass-jawed chump "Toro Moreno" in *The Harder They Fall*. Sylvester Stallone's *Rocky* series looks comic next to these movies, a joke. All of these pictures are grim affairs, tragedies; just like what became of the mumbling, permanently slow-motion Muhammad Ali, dumb brute King Levinsky selling handpainted ties around the swimming pools of Miami Beach hotels, or Sugar Ray Seales who fought four fights while legally blind. You can see it all in these movies.

Colorado Territory (See *High Sierra*)

Conflict

1945. Directed by Curtis Bernhardt. Starring Humphrey Bogart, Alexis Smith, Sydney Greenstreet, Rose Hobart, and Charles Drake.

A pure product of the German Expressionist cinema, with story by Robert Siodmak and directed by Bernhardt, another German refugee. The atmosphere is heavy, ponderous, dark, with lots of rain and misty windows and too much furniture in the rooms. You can feel the closeness indoors, the damp outside. Bogey is as sinister as hell in this. He's in love with his wife's sister, played by Alexis Smith, and wants the wife to divorce him, which she refuses to do, but in a semi-nice way. She's still in love with him and is naturally disturbed that it's her sister he prefers. On the way home from a dinner party at the home of their psychiatrist friend, Sydney Greenstreet, Bogey and his wife have an automobile accident, and he injures his legs. The result is that he's confined to a wheelchair, but even after he recovers and can walk all right again, he conceals his condition and keeps using the wheelchair.

His reason becomes obvious: he decides to murder his wife

in such a way that nobody will suspect he did it. When his wife leaves in her car for a holiday at a mountain resort, Bogey ambushes her at a turn in the road, hobbles out of the shadows and strangles her. Then he dumps her car over a cliff and beats it back home. Now the problems start: he keeps feeling her presence, sniffs her perfume, finds pieces of her clothing, jewelry he's certain she'd taken with her. And it wrecks him when the sister decides she can't marry Bogey because of her sister's memory; there'll always be a barrier between them. So now Bogey is really going mad. He sticks to his wheelchair, and goes to see Greenstreet to get some advice about his mental state. He's sure his wife is still alive. Sydney assures him it's all in his head, that Katherine (the wife) did, indeed, perish in the accident. But Bogey even sees her in the street!

Bogey blows it by returning to the scene of the crime. In the meantime, Greenstreet realizes that when Bogey described Katherine at the moment he last saw her, he mentioned the rose she was wearing. Greenstreet knows something's up now because it was he who had given Katherine the rose after she'd left home and stopped by to see him; she'd then continued on her way up the mountain. Bogey could not have known she was wearing a rose unless he'd seen her after that! So Greenstreet rounds up the cops and they ambush Bogey on the mountain the same way he'd waylaid Katherine. They see Bogey walking perfectly well and grab him as he appears to search around the murder site. The mist and shadows curl around them, Bogey sneers and looks frightened at the same time as only he could do.

This movie is like good German potato salad, heavy and spicy at the same time.

Cry Danger

1951. Directed by Robert Parrish. Starring Dick Powell, Rhonda Fleming, William Conrad, Richard Erdman, and Regis Toomey.

Raymond Chandler supposedly said that Dick Powell was the actor closest to his idea of Philip Marlowe, and was happiest with Powell's performance in *Murder, My Sweet*, the first film version of *Farewell, My Lovely*, out of all the movie Marlowes, including Bogart. Powell began his movie career as a song and dance man and became upset with certain critics' pigeonholeing of him as a somewhat effeminate screen presence. He got out from under that label with the Marlowe role and others, including *Cry Danger*, wherein he portrays an ex-con out for revenge on a frame-up.

Featuring the hillier sections of Los Angeles, with some excellent streetcar/crooked buildings/city streets photography by Joseph Biroc, *Cry Danger* is a straightforward, fast-moving, unpretentious movie, a chronicle of High Dudgeon and Low Company. Powell, as Rocky, is released from stir after five years served for murder and robbery. The cops realize belatedly that he was framed, and he's out to clip the culprits himself. But he's a straight arrow, a very moral guy, so he leads the bulls—Regis Toomey (as the detective Cobb) in particular—to the prey, and lets them make things right. But he's not about to forget the five big ones ripped out of his life, and he makes things as miserable as possible for the double-crossers before serving them up.

Rocky's buddy Danny is still in prison, claiming innocence, and Rocky wants to clear him, too. He knows the fat gangster, Castro, played by William Conrad, is responsible for the fall. After Castro plants stolen money on Rocky via a racing bet with a bookie stooge, Rocky makes Castro lie down on his desk and plays one-way Russian Roulette until the fat man confesses. The best by-play of the movie is between Rocky and Danny's wife, Nancy (Rhonda Fleming). Nancy's been sitting on $50,000, half of the stolen loot, for the five years, and doesn't spill the truth to Rocky about Danny having really been in on the score until she begs Rocky to run off with her. Nancy and Rocky were close pals before she married Danny, and of course she's ready to dump Danny now for the Right Guy. Rocky's already been propositioned by another wrong-way dame named Darlene, and he's sick of it. He leads Nancy on only until he's got the story straight, then hands her over to Cobb, too. Nancy lives in a bric-a-brac heaven, a cozy trailer covered by clinging vines. The setting is claustrophobic, and you can see Rocky squirm thinking about life with this devil-woman. He'd rather pal around with his alcoholic counterfeit former Marine buddy Delong, whose disease is on the surface. Rocky is a stand-up guy: next to him everybody in this movie is made to appear shifty, nervous, like they're hiding something. Even the cops seem soiled compared to Powell.

The question here is how Rocky got mixed up with these bad eggs in the first place. Question number two is where he goes from here. For all his purgative behavior Rocky just isn't the type to lose himself in a faceless slave. I'd like to see the sequel.

Cul-de-Sac   (See *Repulsion*)

Cult of the Cobra

1955. Directed by Francis D. Lyon. Starring Faith Domergue, Richard Long, David Janssen, Marshall Thompson, and Jack Kelly.

Now this is really an insane/inane little movie that deserves attention if only for the unexpected, perfect evocation of Greenwich Village bohemian life in the 1950s. It starts out, however, in Southeast Asia, a kind of Hollywood Thailand, where GIs are stationed. A bunch of these dopey guys smuggle themselves into a secret "native" ritual involving a cobra cult in an effort to avail themselves of some genuine local action. They see things they're not meant to see—things "outsiders" (especially white American soldiers with fraternity boy mentalities) can't properly comprehend, and so they're marked for death when discovered.

Back in the U.S. of A., civilians all, these goofy witnesses to the dark forces of the East are hunted down one by one by the

Cobra Princess, played by Faith Domergue, who somehow manages to look reptilian even in female human being drag. Big, good guy Marshall Thompson falls for her—she's his neighbor in the Village apartment building—but so does his pal Jack Kelly, and she sheds her scales for Richard Long. It's nuts but suspenseful, especially when Domergue transforms herself into a cobra as we watch her shadow on the wall and then slithers out her bedroom window. The scene where she stalks and kills David Janssen in his bowling alley after hours is comparable to Simone Simon tracking and terrorizing Jane Randolph in the darkened basement swimming pool in *Cat People.* Very scary.

But this is a better take on beat life in New York than either the stupid film version of Kerouac's *The Subterraneans* or the nasty-minded *The Beat Generation* by Albert Zugsmith with Ray Danton as a creepy beatnik rapist. Faith Domergue gets to like her life as a hot-blooded woman more than her slimy cobra body; she heats up as a dame and finally can't take the schizophrenia of it all and goes out her apartment window one last time. She drops to the pavement as a snake and is crushed but turns into a woman (somehow in a dress! Wait a minute—who was that cobra wearing a dress?!) so the couple of guys left that she was also supposed to bite to death see her true identity revealed.

The most striking (no pun intended) shots in this snake-*noir* epic are the shadow-on-the-wall ones of Faith's woman-into-cobra transformation. *Cult of the Cobra* is director Francis D. Lyon's great paean to anthropomorphism; sophisticated foolishness that nevertheless conveys a vivid image of psychosexual conflict. I mean, what would you do if every time you got horny you turned into a cobra and bit somebody? This may be a more serious-minded movie than I thought.

The Damned Don't Cry

1950. Directed by Vincent Sherman. Starring Joan Crawford, David Brian, Steve Cochran, Richard Egan, and Kent Smith.

A first-class Crawford tearjerker. Joan's married to an oil-field worker, Richard Egan, happily enough though they're pretty close to dirt-poor. Her parents live with them, and Joan and Dick have a young son, a good kid who's the light of their life. The boy really wants a new bicycle but dad says no, it's too expensive; they hardly have enough money to exist as it is. But Joan wants her boy to be happy and she makes a down payment on the bike. When her husband finds out, he's furious and demands that it be taken back. Joan swears she'll pay for it herself, do extra washing, clean houses for people to make enough money so that it doesn't come out of his pocket. Egan asserts himself mightily and says absolutely not, the bike goes back. The kid goes off on it down the road and gets hit by a tanker truck and dies. That pretty much does it for the marriage. Joan says she can't take it anymore and splits.

In the big city Joan goes to work as a model and is spotted by a big-time gangster, David Brian. She becomes his mistress and gets all the material goodies she's been denied as the faithful, oil-field wife: mink coats, diamonds, Parisian fashions. She becomes a very hot number and has to fend off passes right and left. Even top thug Brian's bookkeeper, Kent Smith (Simone Simon's long-suffering husband in *Cat People*) goes for her. She's on top now and Bakersfield is a lifetime away. Before too long, however, Brian's empire begins to unravel and when the shit really hits the fan Joan has nowhere to run but back to the oil-fields.

When she shows up at the crummy little shack, her parents and abandoned husband Egan don't want her around. She's wearing a full-length fur coat, pearl necklace, rings, diamond earrings, and her hair's in a fancy wave. To them she's a creature from another planet, not their cotton-dress poor-white Joan. The cops want her, Brian's out to kill her, and she ends up on the same road that little Bobby got mashed on. How not feel sorry for this woman, but how blame Egan and the old folks? The problem with Crawford, and Barbara Stanwyck for that matter, is that for me their looks keep me at a distance. I don't want to be involved with these women. I don't go for the truckdriver types, and so I can watch them impassively and not care whether they go off the ledge or not. But this movie works as more than a run-of-the-mill soaper. Somehow it's honest, with genuine conflicts on more than one level. Contrast this with Joseph Pevney's 1955 Crawford-Jeff Chandler vehicle *Female on the Beach,* which doesn't come close to working. In that one Joan is already beyond herself, approaching *Trog* jokedom. The Joan of the '40s was the best, and this is the last of it.

Dark Passage

1947. Directed by Delmer Daves. Screenplay by Delmer Daves and David Goodis; adapted from the novel by David Goodis. Starring Humphrey Bogart, Lauren Bacall, Agnes Moorehead, and Bruce Bennett.

Virtually everything that happens in this movie is silly, far-fetched, or just plain unreal. All of which is perfectly fine—movies aren't meant to *be* real. The reality is in the feelings produced by the viewing. So here we have Agnes Moorehead's best screen performance. She literally vibrates with evil as the murderess Madge Rapf, an arch slut/bitch unlike any other female villain this side of Judith Anderson in *Rebecca.*

Bogey escapes from Santy Q (as San Quentin is called by the cons), having been unjustly sentenced to life for a murder Madge committed (she was jealous of his wife so she killed her). After one aborted ride, the feline Bacall picks up Bogey on a country road. She's convinced he's innocent, and had attended his trial every day. A rich girl. Takes him home. But he can't hide there for long—it turns out Madge knows her, too, and she comes snooping around, sniffing out her new boyfriend Bob (Bruce Bennett) who's stuck on Bacall. Bogey leaves and goes to an underground doctor touted by a cabbie who swears he can make him look like a different man in no time.

The movie is displayed through Bogey's eyes—we never see his face until after the bandages are on except in a newspaper photo, his old face. The new one we see when the bandages come off. The scene with the crazy plastic surgeon at two A.M. whose office is down a dark alley is the best of all, full of distended closeups and warped proportions, like faces leaning over a coffin; and we see them as would a corpse. Everyone looks already-dead, half-faded in failing light. As someone once said of the characters in Goodis's books, there are only two types: the wounded and the slain. The mad doc operates and Bogey goes to see his only pal, a musician who can hide him. But he arrives to find the musician dead, his head bashed in with his trumpet—Madge got there first. So there's no place left to go but Bacall's, and she takes him in. Ties down his hands at night while he sleeps on his back so his fragile face won't get wrecked. Feeds him through a glass straw. They fall for each other, naturally—and it's fun, for real, not a physical attraction on her part because he looks like The Invisible Man.

When the bandages come off he's Bogey, all right. "I look ten years older," he says, "but I'm not." "I think I like you better," says Bacall. Now he goes after Madge, after first disposing of a petty would-be blackmailer, the first guy who picked him up on the run. He pretends to seduce Agnes, then springs the truth on her; she freaks and goes out a window. Bogey makes an improbable escape but he can pass; he's got a different face. He phones Bacall from a bus station booth, tells her where he's headed—a coastal town in Peru. Wait awhile, he says, and if I make it, if you—too many ifs. But, of course, they rendezvous with Bogey in a white tux in a tropical nightclub like *Casablanca* and Bacall slithering across the room toward him like she did in *To Have and Have Not*. Instead of Hoagy Carmichael in the background it's "Too Marvelous for Words," Bogey's grinning like the Cheshire Cat as the warm waves slather the palm-strewn sands, and we fade out to a wonderland where the wounded survive and the wicked don't.

Dead Reckoning

1947. Directed by John Cromwell. Starring Humphrey Bogart, Lizabeth Scott, Morris Carnovsky, and Wallace Ford.

Wallace Ford was in more movies than any other human being. I think that's a fact. In this one he has a small role as an ex-con safecracker who helps Bogey out. But you know the interesting thing about Wallace Ford is that he's *never* wrong for the part. A real professional, physically somewhere between Frank Faylen and John Marley, both of whom he precedes.

Whenever I think of *Dead Reckoning* there are several scenes that leap at me: Bogey holed up in the Old South hotel or whatever it's called, pitching apples or oranges into the couch with a creaky 1920s-style wind-up; Bogey and that bogus Bacall, Lizabeth Scott, streaking along the Gulf of Mexico in a convertible; Bogey's GI buddy running away from the train in the Philly railyards; the neon hotel lights blinking on and off in the humid Tampa night air. This is a very solid movie all the way around. The only person who doesn't completely click is Scott, and she toughs it out, but she's hard to swallow as a nightclub singer—a voice worse than Bacall's. (Come to think of it, both of their singing was probably dubbed.)

Bogey and a war pal are flown to the States from overseas to receive medals for bravery. They're on a train to Washington, D.C., from New York when his friend discovers that there'll be reporters and photographers and newsreel cameras to greet them at the station and at the ceremony later, and he takes a sudden powder. This mystifies Bogey, who goes to the guy's hometown—not identified, but it's Tampa—and tried to get the lowdown on why Johnny ran out on the scene. He finds out Johnny is wanted for a murder—one he didn't commit, of course—and didn't want his mug captured. He'd used a phony name in the service and knew he'd be found out with all the attention. So Bogey takes up with Johnny's old flame, Scott, who's tied in with Carnovsky, the nightclub owner (right out of *Gilda*). Johnny gets whacked before Bogey gets to town, however, which complicates the case, but clears the way for Bogey and the dame to get together.

Movies like this depend on nothing so much as mood, on Bogey's epiphanic expressions, his ability to skate through and around the ham-fisted situations, to make the viewer comfortable through an illusion of competence. Actually, a movie that bears some similarity to this one insofar as *feel* is concerned is Stuart Heisler's odd little *Storm Warning,* made in 1950 with Ronald Reagan and Ginger Rogers. Both movies are without an off-putting degree of pretense and present unusual real-life situations (in *Storm Warning,* Ginger Rogers tries to convince her younger sister that the sister's husband—Steve Cochran—is a Klan member) that engage the viewer gently and soberly and sincerely. It helps to have a presence like Bogey's in there, of course. *Dead Reckoning* is better than the sum of its parts would seem to yield, which is probably due to the soft sea breeze that blows through it.

Desperate

1947. Directed by Anthony Mann. Starring Steve Brodie, Audrey Long, Raymond Burr, Jason Robards, Sr., Douglas Fowley, Paul E. Burns and Ilka Gruning.

My buddy Magic Frank lived next door to me in Chicago with his two older brothers, Woody and Jerry, and their mother. I spent quite a bit of time at their house from the age of ten until I was seventeen, and there were few dull moments. The brothers were constantly hammering on one another and their mother regularly pounded on them. All three boys were bruisers. Mealtime at their house was like a scene out of the movie *One Million B.C.,* in which the cavemen wrestled each other and tore each other's lungs out just to snatch a piece of meat.

The biggest and toughest of the three was the eldest, Jerry, also known as Moose. Moose was a legendary Chicago athlete who had starred in basketball and football in high school and then went on to play tackle and guard at two or three different universities. After the boys' father died, Moose came home and took over the family automobile insurance business, which was failing. Moose decided to specialize in insuring so-called uninsurable motorists, drivers who had been in multiple accidents or had acquired so many moving violation citations that the more regular companies felt they were too poor a risk. The rates Moose charged these people were exhorbitant but if they failed to pay on time Moose attached their property, usually their car, until they came across. If the collateral was insufficient, there would be other, less benign consequences.

Moose's first partner in this enterprise was a six foot tall, 300 pound monster named Cueball Bluestein. Moose was six-three and two-twenty, so they comprised quite a tag team. Cueball was the designated enforcer, although Moose was no slouch if push came to shove came to pull some deadbeat's ear off and mail it to his wife and kids. The boys at Mid-Nite Insurance knew how to do business in Chicago.

Cueball really was a beast, though. Whenever he saw me or Frankie he'd hit us so hard on the arm or shoulder we'd carry the bruise for three weeks. The worst thing was to get caught in a narrow hallway with him where he'd ram his bulk into you against a wall, squeezing out all of your breath, then leave you gasping on the floor while he waddled away, laughing. I hated him, and so did Frank.

After I left the neighborhood I kept in touch with Frankie, and through him I heard news of his brothers, but I didn't know much about what had become of Cueball Bluestein other than that at some point he'd been confined to Clark County, Nevada—which includes Las Vegas—as part of some kind of Mafia deal. I knew Cueball was a big gambler and that he'd become a hit man for the Chicago mob, but I didn't know any of the details until I had dinner with Frank one night in Chicago years later.

According to Frank, after Cueball and Moose parted company in the insurance business—though they remained friends—Cueball went to work for Dodo Saltimbocca, the Chicago crime boss. The night before Saltimbocca was scheduled to testify in front of a commission investigating organized crime, Cueball, who was as close to Saltimbocca as you could get, being his aide and confidant, shot and killed him. The other Chicago bosses thought that Saltimbocca was going to rat on them so they got Cueball to pull the trigger. For this good deed Cueball was sent to Vegas and installed as the number two man under Sammy Eufemia, for whom he labored a number of years. The Chicago mob ruled Vegas and the New York mob ruled Atlantic City and all was, if not entirely copacetic, understood.

The Chicago cops, as well as the Feds, knew that Cueball had murdered Saltimbocca, but the deal was that they wouldn't touch him as long as he remained in Clark County. All went swimmingly until Sammy Eufemia wound up piled on top of his brother, Bitsy, in a shallow grave in an Indiana cornfield. Both Bitsy and Sammy had been shot in the exact same spot in the back of their head. Dodo Saltimbocca had been similarly executed.

Had Cueball made the move in order to become number one in Vegas? Or was it a play on the part of the New York crowd looking to horn in on forbidden territory? Frankie didn't know, he told me, and didn't want to. He did know that Cueball was currently in prison in Nevada on a ten year rap for receiving stolen property, mostly jewelry. On his income tax form each year, Frank said, Cueball always listed his profession as "jeweler."

"He was never a nice guy," I said to Frank.

"True," Frankie said, "but he was from the neighborhood, same as us. Also same as us," said Frank, "his father died when he was young. I'm sure that's one reason I got into as many fights as I did when I was a kid. I was upset."

"Maybe," I said, "but you didn't become a killer, and neither did I."

"Well," said Frank, "probably Cueball was more pissed off about it than we were."

When I saw Anthony Mann's movie *Desperate*, the first of his amazing *noir* trio (*Raw Deal* and *T-Men* are the others), the Raymond Burr character, Walt Radak, immediately reminded me of Cueball Bluestein. Burr is the leader of a group of third-rate gangsters who are in pursuit of a truck driver and his wife in order to frame him for a murder Burr's brother committed. There's one especially outstanding, unnerving, violent scene in which the thugs work over the truckdriver, played by Steve Brodie, in a basement hideout lit only by a hanging lamp. The one-bulb lamp swings crazily and erratically back and forth each time it's knocked into by an arm or shoulder reacting from a blow delivered to the captive Brodie. It's the only light in the place so the men are heavily shadowed, their faces sliced by the knifelike light. The scene is exceptionally brutal but fascinating for the images glancing off and after one another. Burr is the nasty fat man who commands the men with pleasure, as obvious and deadly as Cueball Bluestein.

Detour

1945. Directed by Edgar G. Ulmer. Starring Tom Neal, Ann Savage, and Pat Gleason.

Ulmer made—*dashed-off*—more cheap movies than anyone this side of Roger Corman; he is the prince of under-*noir* (my label). Ulmer's master was F. W. Murnau (*Sunrise, Nosferatu*), and those Prussian shadows shriek throughout his work. His most satisfying homage to Murnau was *The Black Cat* with Lugosi and Karloff, a cranky, crazy-man movie, and he went on to produce junk like *Jive Junction* and *The Naked Dawn*. He even made films in Ukrainian and Hebrew. He's filmdom's directorial Travis Bickle: "I'll make movies anyplace, anytime."

But *Detour,* despite the cruddy, economic ending, is Ulmer's lasting achievement. Tom Neal is perfectly cast as the dumbshit dupe who thinks he knows what he's doing. Ann Savage (née Bernie Lyon!) gives a *tour de force* performance as the tubercular madwoman manipulating Neal to Total Loss. They're right up there with John Dall and Peggy Cummins in *Gun Crazy* in the Looney Tunes department. Neal is an unhappy nightclub musician in New York (Ulmer gives us a hokey long walk up Riverside Drive in the fog that's A-1 in the dry ice category) who decides to hitchhike across the country to meet up with his fiancée in Los Angeles. He can't live without her so he gives up his solid gig and suffers through the tortures of the road dreaming of that blonde pussy at the end of the trail. Kerouac and Cassady were better prepared for the highway than this guy: by the time Neal hits Arizona he's totally broke and wasted looking. A Miami bookie named Haskell picks him up, stakes him to a meal, and shows him the scars on his wrist: an old one from a saber fight from when he was a kid ("I put out the other kid's eye."), and two fresh ones from a dame he picked up on the road a while back ("You give a girl a lift you expect a little something in return. Right, bud?").

Haskell collapses and dies from a bad heart or something so Neal, thinking he'll be suspected of murder, shoves the guy out, takes his clothes, money, I.D., and car. Near Needles he offers a ride to a woman with her thumb out at a gas station. It's Ann Savage, the insane chick who scratched Haskell. She spots Neal as an imposter and proceeds to threaten to expose him to the cops unless he sticks with her. Her head is like a bowling pin with brown hair and heavy eyebrows painted on. She's sick, she's a drunk; she's also a sex-beast who tries to seduce Neal. But he's revolted, stupid as he is, and doesn't want any part of her. He can't talk to his fiancée until he splits from Savage. They rent a room to wait till morning when they can flog the heap. Neal knows Savage is nuts but he's got to obey her. He tries to sell the car but can't answer the used car dealer's question about insurance. Savage saves him by saying they don't want to sell it anyway, which confuses Neal. She explains that Haskell's old man was a multimillionaire who's dying—she reads it in the morning paper—and she wants Neal to impersonate Haskell and try to get the inheritance.

O.K., it's crazy, but so is she, and Neal stupidly allows her to drag him back to the apartment where she coughs—he calls her "Camille"—and practically begs him to fuck her. She looks like a deranged leopard stalking off to the bedroom with the telephone to call the cops on him. Neal tries to break the wire but it gets caught around her throat and strangles her. Now he's really a killer, and he takes to the road again, headed nowhere, fiancée forsaken.

Neal's real life was even worse. All the lines in *Detour* about fate, about bad luck and trouble, and death around the corner could have described his own situation. Neal made headlines and fractured his movie career by beating up Franchot Tone in an argument over actress Barbara Payton, who then married Tone, left him a few months later, and took up again with Neal. Then Neal murdered his third wife, Gail Evatt, got convicted of involuntary manslaughter and did six years. He died soon after being released from prison. The almost ultraviolet bands of light across Neal's face in Ulmer's film are like streaks of evil. He tells the story of his comedown sitting in a diner straight out of an Edward Hopper painting, foretelling his own hellish spiral from rich-kid Northwestern and Harvard University grad to Hollywood lout and wifeslayer. Even the daylight in this movie is cloudy. That only three-and-a-half days were taken to edit the film is obvious: Neal is caught hitchhiking with his left hand on the wrong side of the road with the steering wheel on the right side of the car. The moral copout at the finish will make you want to toss your beer can at the screen, but this seamy insanity is worth sixty-three of the sixty-four minutes. One strange thing: current young actor Kurt Russell is a dead ringer for Tom Neal.

The Devil Thumbs a Ride

1947. Directed by Felix Feist. Screenplay by Felix Feist; based on the novel by Robert C. DuSoe. Starring Lawrence Tierney, Ted North, Nan Leslie, and Betty Lawford.

I got up at 3:30 in the morning to watch this movie on T.V.—the perfect time for it. The hours covered in the film are from midnight to dawn, the period during which reality is suspended, when the rational mind loses control, and everything goes haywire. This is one of the meanest, most boldly deranged exercises in maniacal behavior this side of Farmer Ed Gein, minus the dismemberment.

Lawrence Tierney is at his most vicious and amoral here. He robs and murders a theater manager in San Diego, then grabs a lift from a traveling salesman played by Ted North, a decent enough, slightly tipsy, average Joe on his way home to the little woman in L.A. Tierney, famous for his role as Dillinger for Robert Wise in 1945, and for his barroom brawls (he was stabbed in one as recently as 1973), and drunk driving arrests, is the wickedest looking big lug in B-movie history. He dresses sharp. He's got big shoulders and a snap brim fedora; evil doesn't lurk in his face, it gloats. He's a real con man, convincing the salesman, named Furgison—"Furgie" he calls him—to let him drive, that way they'll get to Los Angeles faster and safer. Right. At a gas station in Oceanside two young women approach the car. They'd met in Globe, Arizona, hitched a ride to San Diego, and are now hitching their way up the coast highway, just looking for a lift. Tierney says sure, hop in. Furgie doesn't like it—he's married, you know. How will anyone know? asks Tierney. Furgie agrees. Tierney arranges it to suit himself: the brassy blonde up front with Furgie, the better-looking brunette in the back seat with him.

Before they leave the filling station, though, Tierney insults the attendant when he shows Furgie a picture of his two-year-old kid. With those ears the kid could be a flier, says the Mean Big Guy. The attendant pays special notice to Tierney, and after they drive off he hears a description of Furgie's car, a gray convertible, on the police band: the car was spotted driving away from the scene of the robbery. The gas jockey runs to the cops, of course, and an APB goes out all the way up the coast to L.A. The kid goes along with a detective from Oceanside to help in the chase, to identify Tierney.

In the car Tierney comes on hard and fast to the brunette, telling her about his Hollywood connections, how a girl like her, with perfect lips, eyes, legs, should be a movie star; he can help her out. He frightens her but she's interested. The brassy one up front is the bad one and Tierney spots it; he likes the innocent, naïve soul to chew up and spit out. They stop at a roadside diner but there's a roadblock ahead. Tierney rushes them all back to the car, takes the wheel and peels out, headed for a road off the highway to get around the blockade. A motorcycle cop comes after them—the cop puts on his sunglasses, at two-thirty/three A.M.!—and Tierney backs up into him, crushing his leg. The cop fires a few rounds at the speeding gray car, but Tierney gets away.

By now Furgie knows he's in trouble, but he's told Tierney about a beach house a friend of his keeps and they head there, to Newport. Don't worry about that cop back there, Tierney tells Furgie. He couldn't be too badly hurt; after all, he fired three shots after I ran him over, didn't he? So the monster and the girls take over the beach house. The old night watchman comes in and Tierney gets him drunk so that he passes out. Furgie phones his wife who hears the blonde laughing and music from the radio and hangs up on him. Furgie runs out to find someone to drive him to L.A. right away, but his car has two flat tires now, cut up by Tierney with broken whiskey bottles. Tierney terrorizes the brunette, chases her down to the beach where he beats her up and she drowns in the shallows by the pier. Meanwhile, the cops are mobilized from Dago to San Clemente. The blonde fixes herself some food and takes over a bedroom. Furgie comes back, sweating, crazed, and opens her door. Boy, she says, I'm improving my mind. She holds up a book. "Who is this guy Balzac?" she asks. "He sure can write."

Furgie's life has gone to hell, dragged down step by step by the massive-shouldered devil Tierney. The beach house is a wreck. Don't worry, Tierney tells him, conning him again, everything'll be fixed up like new. Tierney steals Furgie's wallet, his money, and I.D. The cops break in and Tierney pretends that he's Furgie, shows the I.D., imitates Furgie's signature, and almost gets away with it until the detective and the filling station kid come in and the kid fingers Tierney. The cops find the floating brunette. Tierney tears the place up and beats it out to the cop car with the blonde. They get away as daylight breaks. A patrol car chases them down outside Santa Ana and shoots them both dead. The sun comes out of the fog. Furgie's wife arrives from L.A., frantic, but he calms her. All is well. She's pregnant, she says. They laugh and embrace. The night has ended.

The Devil Thumbs a Ride is as frenzied as *Gun Crazy*, as darkly depraved as *Detour*, but simpler, more linear. (Felix Feist made only one other halfway decent film, *This Woman is Dangerous*, a 1952 gun moll-crying towel vehicle for Joan Crawford.) Tierney invests this basically stupid plot with such genuine virulence that *Devil* must be ranked in the upper echelon of indelibly American *noir*. I saw Tierney on an episode of "Hill Street Blues" not long ago, and in Norman Mailer's *Tough Guys Don't Dance* (1987), a movie he steals with ease. He's in his sixties now, fat, and completely bald. His gigantic, gleaming skull is absolutely square. In "Hill Street" he played an old police sergeant and he didn't have many lines, but that mean look was still in his eyes; that bad-to-the-bone, never-give-in visage. There is no daylight in that face.

D.O.A.

1949. Directed by Rudolph Maté. Starring Edmond O'Brien, Pamela Britton, Luther Adler, and Neville Brand.

What if you woke up one day in a strange city, felt a little queasy, went to a doctor, and he told you you had only several days or hours to live? What would *you* do? Edmond O'Brien spends his precious little time trying to find out who poisoned him and why. I don't think I would, but who knows?

D.O.A. is one of the fastest paced, most uncompromising nightmares on celluloid. Rudy Maté, born in Krakow, schooled in Budapest, apprenticed as a cinematographer to Korda, Freund, Pommer, Carl Dreyer (*Vampyr*, 1932), Fritz Lang, René Clair, and Ernst Lubitsch (who could ask for more?!), directed this ultra-*noir* masterpiece, a movie that has everyone in a violent sweat from beginning to end. O'Brien's an insurance man in a small California desert town. He needs a few days away from his fiancée, played by Pamela Britton (a not-quite-pretty blonde), who's hounding him to set a date. O'Brien's nervous, needs a drink too early in the day. He goes to San Francisco, stays at the St. Francis and falls in with some conventioneers and their wives, one of whom makes a serious pass at him. He ditches them and tries to pick up a hip chick at the bar of a prebeatnik jazz bar, The Fisherman. There's a great scene here: closeups of the sweating sax player, a ringer for Bird, eyes bulging, tilted frame—Maté utilizing all his Expressionist tricks. While the sound rises and the customers get frantic, a tall figure in an overcoat with a turned-up checkered collar and slouch hat, face hidden, drops something in a drink and switches it with O'Brien's. The mysterious stranger ducks out while O'Brien hustles the frail. She puts him off till later, gives him a number on a piece of paper. "Call me there in a little while," she says. O'Brien takes a slug from his glass, chokes, coughs, and tells the bartender to give him another: that one's no good.

He never does hook up with the hipster, talks on the phone instead to his fiancée back in the desert. She's also his secretary and she tells him about a man in L.A. who's been trying to get in touch. O'Brien feels guilty about being in S.F. chasing dames behind her back, goes to sleep. In the morning he feels funny, stomach's upset. A doctor tells him he's in good shape but then checks the X-ray: luminous poison in his system, a dead man. O'Brien freaks, runs all over town, finally to the old Southern Pacific hospital on Fell Street. A doc there confirms the diagnosis. How? Why? He goes back to The Fisherman; it's closed. He looks at a child on the street. No future now, barely a present. He calls the guy in L.A. who was desperate to talk to him. The man's dead. O'Brien flies to L.A., finds out the guy was poisoned the same way, a guy O'Brien had notarized a paper for, a contract, nothing big, a chance meeting. But something was wrong with the deal and O'Brien, the witness, had to go too. He dashes to the cops, who are on the lookout for him. "I want to report a murder," he tells them. "Whose?" they ask. "Mine," O'Brien says.

Maté uses the city streets brilliantly in this, making it all into a maze with O'Brien the frightened, maddened, careening rabbit slamming into the wall with nothing making sense. Sweat, sweat, sweat—this movie has it. All improbable, impossible, with finger-snapping blondes, bop, post-World War Two '50s-prosperous American city scenes twisted through the bottom of a glass by an uncompromising, Kandinskylike eye. Remade in 1969 as *Color Me Dead*, a dud. Maté's is the one to see.

Double Indemnity

1944. Directed by Billy Wilder. Screenplay by Raymond Chandler and Billy Wilder, based on the novel by James M. Cain. Starring Fred MacMurray, Barbara Stanwyck, Edward G. Robinson, Byron Barr, Jean Heather, and Tom Powers.

I've always been fascinated by the use of Barbara Stanwyck as a femme fatale in the movies. She does nothing for me. For her to have been paired in *Double Indemnity* with Fred MacMurray, whom I consider to be the male equivalent to Stanwyck, makes sense. Neither of them seem attractive enough on the surface to be quite the person they *want* to be. They do a good job of pretending that the other is the genuine object of their affection, or object of their genuine affection, one or both. As Walter Neff, the insurance agent who crosses over and teams up with the evil Phyllis Dietrichson to murder her husband and collect on his accident policy, MacMurray appears neither as charmed by her as we're meant to believe, nor as stupid as he has to be to go in on the deal. But the movie is magnificent nonetheless, if only for Edward G. Robinson's performance as Keyes, Neff's superior, a dogged investigator for whom Neff has great affection and respect, and who busts the case so that both Neff and Phyllis go down for the long count.

James M. Cain based his story on an actual case from the 1920s. He liked writing about triangle murders, and excellent films were made of his *The Postman Always Rings Twice* (the first one, not the second), *Mildred Pierce*, and *Double Indemnity*. His finest novel, however, *Serenade*, was horribly butchered by director Anthony Mann in 1956 and starred Mario Lanza (Elvis Presley's idol) in a semimusical version. Wilder and Chandler kept the cynicism intact in *Double Indemnity*, though; the cruel part is when Neff finds out that the character Nino Zachette is not really Phyllis's daughter Lola's love, but her own. Neff is the perfect dupe, the ideal guy who knows the insurance business from the inside out. Who better for Phyllis to seduce into being her accomplice? It's all very ingenious and dark; there's no real sentimentality in this. The most touching scene is reserved for the two men, Neff and Keyes, when Neff is dying and Keyes, for whom Neff has been lighting cigars throughout the picture, lights Neff's final cigarette. Robinson is the most sympathetic character in the movie, despite the fact that he's the hardnose, impossible-to-fool chief claims investigator. That he so obviously enjoys his work—he brings a genuine zest to the activities—makes the duplicitous, shadowy ways of the others appear even more odious than usual. Keyes is serious but sympathetic, friendly, decent. MacMurray and Stanwyck are severely compromised individuals, derailed losers whose selfishness seals their doom.

The lighting is of primary importance in this movie, especially the interior of Phyllis's house when she meets Neff there: the slanting, ugly shadows reflect each of their souls. And there's a priceless scene when her crippled husband is shoved off the rear of a moving train. All the smiles in this one are of the crocodile variety except for Edward G.'s.

Edge of the City

1957. Directed by Martin Ritt. Screenplay by Robert Allan Arrthur. Starring John Cassavetes, Sidney Poitier, Jack Warden, and Ruby Dee.

Martin Ritt's first feature film. To paraphrase Georges Sadoul, Ritt never came close to duplicating this feat. *Edge of the City* is as powerful as *On the Waterfront*, to which it owes some debts. Nevertheless it stands on its own. It's edited by Sidney Meyers, who tutored Cassavetes and influenced him in his own directorial career (especially *Shadows*). A brave movie, dealing with interracial relationships, Poitier emerges as the hero, the sane *savant* amidst cruel city animals.

Smoky black and white. Cassavetes, still a goodlooking young punk, fresh off *Crime in the Streets*, is an army deserter living in a dumpy room and working on the New York docks as a longshoreman. He's befriended by Poitier, who takes him home to meet his sweet wife, Ruby Dee, and his little son in the housing project.

Cassavetes is paranoid, cold, on the run. Calls his mother back in Indiana but can't talk, afraid the line's tapped, he'll be caught. "Axel! Axel!" she cries. "Is that you?" Changes his last name from Nordstrom to North. But Poitier loosens him up a bit, introduces him to a (white) softspoken chick, a social-worker, wallflower type, whom Cassavetes briefly romances. With Sid and Ruby they play bop records, dance in the living room, drink beer. A nice '50s-hip scene.

But then things break at the docks. Jack Warden plays the mean bully foreman who forces Sid into a fight with hooks, baiting him. Poitier's hook gets caught in a wire screen and Warden, the big lug Irishman, hooks him in the back. Sid dies, Axel swears revenge, even though it means he'll be caught as a deserter. Now Cassavetes's hatred spills out, the months on the run, frustration, enormous sadness, his one friend dead. Nobody else will tell the truth, confront the foreman—they're all afraid. But Axel faces him down, the short, wiry, leather-jacketed Scandinavian kid, doomed against the beefy, broken-nosed, red-faced potatohead.

The workers gather, hypnotized by the crazed, intense scene. Cassavetes is mad-eyed, wild with rage; Warden, desperate and hateful. He knows he has to kill Cassavetes to preserve the fiction that Sid's death was an accident. They go at it with hooks, the lithe Axel escaping each bull-lunge by jumping crates, taking cat-swipes to keep position. The other workers stay back, suppressed hatred for the foreman now exposed, and they threaten the company goons, the union racketeers, so they'll keep out of it.

The showdown finishes when the foreman rushes for the thrust to crush Cassavetes but stumbles, and Axel's nervous slice sends him down with a thud, dead as Sid. Cassavetes, still crazed, drags the body down the railroad tracks alongside the docks straight into the sustained camera closeup, superhuman, beyond reach.

Finger Man

1955. Directed by Harold Schuster. Starring Frank Lovejoy, Forrest Tucker, Peggie Castle, and Timothy Carey.

I must have first seen Timothy Carey in one of those low-budget 1950s movies, playing a heavy as he does in *Finger Man.* The first two films I can actually remember him in, however, are *One-Eyed Jacks* (1961) with Marlon Brando, where he played a stupid, womanpawing thug, his only lines snarls; and one of the idiotic Beach Blanket epics of the early '60s, with Carey as a drooling, leering goon named South Dakota Slim. Later, of course, John Cassavetes used him in *Minnie and Moskowitz* and *The Killing of a Chinese Bookie,* both small roles; but the opening scene in *Minnie,* the only one shot in New York, where Carey monologizes in a diner, is worth seeing the film for. Even in *Finger Man* he's nothing more than a snarling brute, but an effective one. And that's the point: at what he does, Timothy Carey is *non-pareil.* He's a bizarre screen presence, a Neanderthal-like hulk in modern dress; frightening.

Carey makes *Finger Man* interesting. The shots of him stalking Frank Lovejoy, threatening Lovejoy in a restaurant, growling, snarling (Carey is unequaled at The Unbridled Snarl), grabbing women's arms, attempting to grin, are priceless. He plays a thug, naturally, who works for a crime boss played by Forrest Tucker. Lovejoy is a three-time loser who goes over and cooperates as an undercover man for the Treasury Department in order to avoid going up for life. Lovejoy infiltrates Tucker's mob of liquor hijackers and nightclub lowlifes, takes up with a former B-girl of Tucker's and takes The Big Step to turn his life around. He's also got a psycho-alcoholic sister with a little girl that he tries to save, another refugee from Tucker's tentacles. Frank Lovejoy was always a flat actor, pretty much dead in the water. It's not even amusing, really, to watch him interact with Forrest Tucker, another woodenhead, in this one. The women rave and rant and snicker and spark a little, but these guys, along with the Treasury cops, are lifeless.

Lovejoy had his best days in certain camp (read: unintentionally funny) exercises such as *Shack Out on 101*, *I Was a Communist for the FBI*, and occasionally in his television series *Meet McGraw*. He was sturdy-jawed, serious-browed, unflappable, and awfully damn dull. Nobody can take seriously his romantic moments, especially in *Finger Man*; there's no life in his lips, nothing a woman can go for. His suits don't even fit right. Paired as he is in this one with Forrest Tucker, they battle it out for Most Inanimate Male In A So-Called Moving Picture.

What transpires according to the script doesn't mean a thing and is barely worth following. It's Timothy Carey who takes the cake. He's spooky, menacing, ugly; a deranged gorilla in a coat and hat. He slobbers, and can't control his hands or his hair, which keeps falling in his face. Some of the photography here is interesting: low angle approach shots and the odd tilted street keep it visually intriguing. The men in this movie are crude, mean, stupid; the women exploited, stunted, abused. Nothing pretty here except for the stagey ending meant to be scoffed at. Timothy Carey justifies the French intellectual's image of the typical American male.

A Flash of Green (see *The Mean Season*)

The 400 Blows

1959. Directed and written by François Truffaut. Starring Jean-Pierre Leaud, Patrick Auffray, Claire Maurier and Albert Remy.

When I was a boy my mother and I went to movies together often. She loved going to the movies, day or night, all kinds, but especially foreign films: French, British, even Hungarian; movies she couldn't get other adults to see with her, so she took me.

I saw *The 400 Blows* with my mother in 1959, when I was twelve years old, the same age as the film's protagonist, played by Jean-Pierre Leaud. Apparently largely autobiographical, *The 400 Blows* is about a semidelinquent kid who lives in a rundown walkup apartment in Paris with his mother and father. The father is a rather ineffectual, nondescript type, who works a boring nine-to-five job and isn't around much. The mother is a kind of sexy, frustrated blonde who figures the world owes her a better deal. She cheats on her husband, and one afternoon, when the boy is playing hooky, he spots his mother in the street kissing a man. The boy and his mother lock eyes but don't speak, and later she makes a deal with him: she won't say anything about his cutting school if he keeps quiet about what he saw. This disgusts the kid, but what can he do?

There is one scene in the movie that affected me more than any other. The boy and his parents are returning home from a rare family outing, probably on Sunday evening, and as the mother is hanging up her coat in the hallway, her husband reaches up from behind and squeezes her breasts. I remember thinking when I saw this that my mother was a pretty good sport to be taking me to a movie that had stuff like that in it. But I also saw the uncomfortable look on the woman's face when it happened. She didn't like her husband touching her any longer in that intimate way; she was annoyed but tried not to show it, to disguise her unhappiness and disappointment with her marriage, her life. The woman no longer loved her husband, but he loved her, and it was a pathetic moment. I was over-whelmed by an unexpected sadness, a deeply painful feeling for which I was unprepared.

I suppose I identified to a certain extent with the boy, and I saw something of my own mother in the woman on the screen, but somehow that one pathetic gesture on the part of the un-loved, betrayed husband provided me a window on the lie, and revealed the undeniable tragedy inherent in the life yet to come.

The Friends of Eddie Coyle

(see *The Mean Season*)

Get Carter

1971. Directed by Mike Hodges. Starring Michael Caine, Ian Hendry, Britt Ekland, and John Osborne.

An underrated, seldom-mentioned *noir* masterpiece, Mike Hodges's *Get Carter* is the shiny suit of British cinema. Carter (Caine) is a London gangster who finds out his brother has been offed back home in Newcastle. We get a brief glimpse of Carter's chums and digs in London before he hies himself off to the North; we know he's screwing Ekland, who's mistress of the local boss, and that he's a well-respected tough nut. The color's dark, murky in London, and in Newcastle it gets watery, runny, and bland. England looks bleak here, and its inhabitants, exem-plified by Carter and company, seedy and nasty. It's the lower depths striving to look respectable and it doesn't work.

They know it, too. The moment Carter sets foot in town the Newcastle hoods are on his case. He rents a room from a whor-ish landlady, whom he taunts and excites by making a phone call to Ekland in her presence, instructing Ekland to masturbate while he coos into the phone. This disconcerts not only the landlady—who, of course, Carter soon beds—but Ekland's boy-friend who catches her at it. The movie is full of this kinky stuff. When the Newcastle mob boys roust Carter as he's having it off with the landlady, he grabs a double-barreled shotgun from under the bed and marches the thugs out into the street in front of the house without bothering to put on his clothes. A parade is going by at the time and the old woman on her porch next door keels over at the sight. Carter doesn't flinch, just makes certain the baddies exit. There's also an aborted sex scene with Carter and the old lady of the local crime boss—seedily portrayed by British playwright John Osborne—whereat Carter discovers his niece, who may in reality be his daughter, in a porno film produced by the mob.

Carter's brother's been whacked by Osborne's guys, obviously, because he knew too much, even though he was a small-time bloke. Carter figures it out right away but has to go through a series of evening up exercises like locking Osborne's mistress in the trunk of her own car just before the brutes unwittingly dump it in the river. She's no bloody good, Carter's expression says, let her go. It's a cold shot movie, with Caine cruel, clever, and deliberate. *Get Carter* is the movie Peckinpah's version of Jim Thompson's *The Getaway* should have been. McQueen wasn't the actor Caine is, though; he was less subtle and gave everything away with that hang-dog look. Caine has more than two expressions, that's the real difference.

Hodges has the action raw and quick: Carter's either fucking, shooting, throwing somebody off a roof, or observing. You can see his brain registering and computing and plotting. After he's gone too far, gotten too close, Osborne finds a way to have Carter killed, but by the time it happens, on a lonely beach—Carter having accomplished what he came for really—it's already over. We don't *like* Carter—he's a sociopathic, perverse murderer—but we respect his lack of pretense. He may not like himself, either, but he's got his self-respect. Life is for shit, he seems to be thinking, but there's a certain fascination in watching people try to wipe it off.

The Getaway

1972. Directed by Sam Peckinpah. Based on the novel by Jim Thompson. Starring Steve McQueen, Ali McGraw, Ben Johnson, Sally Struthers, Al Lettieri, and Slim Pickens.

A shadow of what it could have been, Peckinpah's version of the great Jim Thompson's novel, *The Getaway*, is nevertheless good entertainment with a few remarkable scenes. Thompson wrote his own script for this movie, which Peckinpah declined to make, hiring instead the veteran script merchant Stirling Silliphant. The most obvious problem for anyone who's read the novel is the ending, which leaves out Thompson's exquisitely surreal denouement, the element that ultimately differentiates his book from any other crime story.

Oh well. Thompson disliked this movie, by the way. But it's worth watching for the bravura performance of Al Lettieri, who played a similar role in *Mr. Majestyk.* McQueen is Doc McCoy, sprung from prison by big shot Ben Johnson after Doc's wife, Carol (Ali McGraw), does him a sexual favor. Doc is an expert on big-time heists (all the experts are in the Big House, right?), and Johnson needs him to come in on a deal. After it's done the money becomes a problem, as always, and Doc and Carol end up running with it, pursued by Lettieri, whom they think has been killed. Lettieri has a great sequence here after he kidnaps a veterinarian and his wife, Sally Struthers, and has them drive him (he's wounded) after Doc. Lettieri turns Struthers on and she strokes his big gun and waves it (and her big tits) in his face and flaunts her partiality for the tough thug Lettieri over her milquetoast husband. Al and Sally slam each other around and the poor vet hangs himself in a motel room.

In the meantime, Carol manages to lose the satchel of money to a grifter in a train station (played with beautiful vulnerability by Richard Bright), and Doc has to go after him and get it back. Then Carol and Doc end up in a garbage dumpster and are hauled out to the city dump and covered, cut and bleeding, by crap. This is a savage shot: Ali McGraw's carefully manicured, cool look totally besmirched by filth—the kind of scene Peckinpah drools over. The showdown comes in a cheap hotel in the Southwest with Doc shotgunning several guys before running out of steam. Carol gets back at the gross cowboy brute Ben Johnson, too, with a deft shot we're not sure is meant for Doc or Ben; she waits until the last instant to make up her own mind. The problem with McGraw is that she's too bland; if she hadn't been McQueen's wife one doubts that she would have been in this movie at all.

Lettieri and Struthers actually steal the show from McQueen and McGraw; they make the exercise worthwhile and really seamy. McQueen, though, is a good Doc McCoy; but the real Doc wouldn't have stuck with this Carol, she's from the wrong neighborhood. If you do see this one make sure you read Thompson's novel to get the real ending. Nobody was better than Jim Thompson at devising hells on earth.

Gilda

1946. Directed by Charles Vidor. Starring Rita Hayworth, Glenn Ford, George Macready, and Joseph Calleia.

Gilda is one of a kind, a masterpiece as gripping if not as clean and well-proportioned as *Sunset Boulevard*; or as purposefully *noir* as, say, *Touch of Evil*. We see Rita at her very best in this; she does her strip number, "Put The Blame On Mame," and gets to twirl her red hair and flaunt her magnificent frame without interruption. Not even the plot gets in the way. Set in Buenos Aires, Glenn Ford is a cynical, down on his luck gambler who uses loaded dice to win at craps in a waterfront game. A guy tries to rob him but Ford is rescued by a stranger wielding a cane and a dagger. Turns out his savior is a gambling/nightclub owner named Mundson, who hires Ford as his righthand man. Ford dedicates himself to Mundson, not knowing he's a Nazi sympathizer and fronts for the Germans in business deals. Everything goes well until Mundson returns from a trip with a wife, played by Rita (Gilda). A couple of things are wrong here: one, Ford resents Mundson's getting married without telling him (Why? Does Ford have sexual feelings toward Mundson?); and two, Ford and Gilda had an affair some time back and Gilda dumped him. Things fall apart.

When Mundson finds out about Ford and Rita's past, he gets jealous and assigns Ford to keep an eye on her. Ford doesn't like the whole deal and wants to split, but he's loyal to his boss, who helped him when he was down. Rita wants to resume relations with Ford but he won't have it, so she goes looney and starts running around town wantonly, really embarrassing Mundson with her "Mame" striptease song and dance. Mundson kills a guy in a fight, comes back to the club, and finds Ford struggling with a drunken Rita. Mundson figures they're lovers again and runs off, supposedly taking a plane that crashes. With Mundson dead, Ford and Rita get married, but Ford is filled with guilt about betraying Mundson and tortures Rita psychologically. She's not going to sit still for that and takes off, working as an entertainer in another city. Ford has her brought back and they reconcile, realizing that they're made for each other. Then things get complicated as Mundson shows up, and he wants to put things back the way they were in the first place; but Rita's pal, the nightclub janitor, shoots Mundson, leaving Glenn and Rita to themselves.

Rita Hayworth comes off best in the movie as a woman knocked around by life, battered by men's expectations of who and what she should be. Ford is a confused man, a guy one step from the gutter when he's rescued by the Nazi nightclub baron. And the guy's a mental case, a power freak. This all adds up to constant conflict and high energy grappling. Nobody's happy or even has any idea of what it might be like to be happy, so they're each out to punish the other guy more than they're being punished themselves. Or maybe it's the other way around and they're a pack of flamboyant masochists, victims of child abuse, broken homes, chemical imbalances, improper diets. Who knows? It's enough just to watch Rita in all her glory descend a winding staircase, to fluff up her hair with one hand and let it fall all over her face while her ears and eyebrows twitch and Macready's nose goes out of joint. Sure, she's saying, blame everything on me you silly boys. *Gilda* is delightfully tawdry, a world-view worth further examination.

Gun Crazy

1949. Directed by Joseph H. Lewis. Starring John Dall and Peggy Cummins.

My friend Steve Fagin thinks that *Gun Crazy* is the greatest American movie ever made. It was Fagin who made me watch it and I'm not sorry I did. This is a bizarre story of a boy who falls in love with guns, and then in love with a girl who loves guns who drives him absolutely nuts.

A kid is fascinated by guns, even breaks a shop window to steal some dueling pistols, and he's caught by the local cop. He's a good kid, really, who just happens to have this yen for iron. He goes into the army, where of course he's a sharpshooter, and when he gets out he goes with his old hometown buddies to a carnival one night. At the carnival he meets a female sharpshooter with a British accent, blonde hair, and a cute ass. They go for each other right away and it's the beginning of the end for him.

The guy—long, tall John Dall, kind of a horse-faced Gary Cooper—has to wrest the platinum Peggy Cummins away from the carnival owner. I forget whether or not they have to kill him but they soon take off on their own. She gets tired of the peanuts they make with their marksman-woman act and suggests they pull a bank job. There's a brilliant sequence where a camera is set on the trunk of their convertible and there's no break in the scene; we're in the backseat with them as they arrive and make their getaway from the bank. Dall doesn't like any of this—the robberies—but he's as insane about Peggy as he is about guns. They're an off-the-wall Bonnie and Clyde but without the posturing and big budget. This movie was made for next to nothing; that shows but it doesn't matter. The camerawork is wicked, like Peggy's mind; the eye is unblinking, relentless, raking across everything it sees like a claw. It's a hard, mean focus, and I suppose that's Joseph Lewis's trademark: the screen pulsates like an injured nerve, and does again in his 1955 movie, *The Big Combo*. It's a damned nervous picture, like Ulmer's *Detour*; but all the more so for Dall's transformation at the hands of the witch from a decent, easygoing good fella to a sweating, fatigued fugitive. (Director Lewis said in an interview that he purposefully chose a gay actor, John Dall, for this role because he felt that a certain subtle vulnerability would show through.)

Their run eventually takes them back to Dall's hometown, where his sister reluctantly takes them in. But they're soon discovered and have to head for the mountains, the Sierras, and Dall's old pals know exactly where to look. The climactic scene, shot in heavy white fog, is exquisite, startling because of the *visual* quiet—we just hear voices and shots. All in all, a remarkable little movie: sexy, violent, stupid, sad, pretty, tense, strange. More than enough.

The Hidden Room

1949. Directed by Edward Dmytryk. Starring Robert Newton, Sally Gray, and Phil Brown.

Sometimes titled *Obsession*, this is a corker about a jealous husband, Newton, a doctor, who finds out his absolutely beautiful wife is having an affair with another man. Newton kidnaps the guy and hides him in an abandoned building, chained to a wall. Every day he brings a container of acid and slowly fills a bathtub that he intends to murder his cuckholder in. This is a great picture of a rational mind at work, enjoying the anticipation, watching his rival suffer, and there's a good predictable trick ending. The real reason to watch this movie, however, is to see the lovely Sally Gray, a British actress who did not appear in many films (*Dangerous Moonlight* was a good one). Her seeming intelligence is part of her beauty; she has it all over any other celluloid blonde as far as I'm concerned. Robert Newton, as always, is evilly, marvelously mad. Phil Brown could be anybody, and is.

High Sierra

1941. Directed by Raoul Walsh. Screenplay by John Huston and W. R. Burnett based on the novel by W. R. Burnett. Starring Humphrey Bogart, Ida Lupino, Arthur Kennedy, Alan Curtis, Joan Leslie, Henry Travers, Henry Hull, Barton MacLane, and Cornel Wilde.

I Died a Thousand Times

1955. Directed by Stuart Heisler. Screenplay by W. R. Burnett based on his novel *High Sierra.* Starring Jack Palance, Shelley Winters, Lee Marvin, Lori Nelson, Perry Lopez, Lon Chaney, Jr., Gonzales Gonzales, and Richard Davalos.

Colorado Territory

1949. Directed by Raoul Walsh. Based on W. R. Burnett's novel *High Sierra.* Starring Joel McCrea, Dorothy Malone, Virginia Mayo, Henry Hull, and Frank Puglia.

All three of these are the same movie, each based on W. R. Burnett's novel, *High Sierra.* Burnett, in fact, scripted two of them, and Raoul Walsh directed them both. *Colorado Territory* is a western, and doesn't really qualify as *noir*. (In fact, the only truly *noir* western is Nicholas Ray's *Johnny Guitar* [1954], wherein standard crime movie stars Sterling Hayden, Joan Crawford, and Ernest Borgnine look pretty funny running around in cowpoke clothes.) Joel McCrea kind of stumbles through this one, though he always looks good as a cowboy; and Henry Hull, who appeared as Doc Banton in *Sierra*, has a reprise in *Territory*.

Director Walsh and writer Burnett made the most out of this story of an escaped convict who ends up being gunned down in the mountains—certainly Burnett may be one of the only writers who succeeded in having the same novel filmed three times in fourteen years! But Walsh turned in the best job on the original: Bogart's famous performance as Mad Dog Roy Earle is notable because it's the fourth time he played an escaped con—the first was his role as Duke Mantee in *The Petrified Forest* (1936)—and he had virtually the same haircut each time: buzz-cut sides and wispy top. He and Ida Lupino make a compelling pair in *Sierra*, both wanting something and someone neither will get. Roy Earle is paroled from prison and heads for California in order to rob a resort hotel. He meets a family traveling west who have a pretty but crippled daughter named Velma. Roy falls for her and promises to try to help her out and get her an operation on her club foot, then goes off to join the mugs sent by Big Mac, Roy's sponsor, to do the job. One of the mugs has brought along a B-girl named Marie, played by Lupino (Shelley Winters, who plays the same role in *I Died a Thousand Times*, is always too fragile-hysterical for my taste). Roy doesn't like a dame around but Marie goes for the guy, even with that crazy haircut. Roy's crazy about Velma and makes sure her family has the money to help her and sets them up with a doctor to perform the operation. Then he stages the holdup, wherein his cohorts are killed, so he and Marie and a dog take off together.

Naturally, Roy goes to see Velma, but now that she's cured and can dance, she rejects Roy, telling him she's not in love with him and has a cute young hunk already hot for her. This devastates Roy, but faithful Marie is right there, and he gives her an engagement ring he'd intended for Velma. Velma's pop, played wincingly by Henry Travers, says, Sorry Roy, what can you do? So Roy and Marie hightail it, the cops in hot pursuit because their inside man at the hotel has spilled the beans. At a motel Roy and Marie see a newspaper with "Mad Dog" splashed all over the front page. This Mad Dog label really riles Roy, and Bogey gets to grit his teeth a lot, to unleash his magnificent half-snarl. He packs off Marie and the little doggie on a bus and heads for the hills. When he gets pinned down on a mountaintop,

Marie returns with the dog, who leaps out of her arms and runs to Bogey who's then drilled into immortality by the bulls.

Bogey is the definitive Mad Dog Roy Earle; he has a certain softness and an almost bland demeanor that smacks of reality, something that Jack Palance, in his Earle effort, cannot for the life of him convey. But Lee Marvin and Earl Holliman as Palance's sidekicks are the perfect gooney yokels—too stupid to live very long. *High Sierra* is more of a tearjerker than *I Died a Thousand Times*, but it's still more plausible somehow. Also, *Sierra* is in black and white so the actors aren't dwarfed by the colorful magnificence of the mountains as they are in *I Died*. I suppose I like *Sierra* better because of Lupino and Henry Travers, both of whom always played characters I figured I'd like to know. An interesting sidenote: Perry Lopez, who played the squealing hotel employee in *I Died*, later turned up as the L.A. cop Escobar in *Chinatown*.

House of Games

1988. Directed and written by David Mamet. Starring Lindsay Crouse and Joe Mantegna.

This is a post-modern/neo-noir (choose one) melodrama dressed up as a morality play. In fact, it is a play, dressed up as a movie—but it's a good one; maybe better than good. Crouse is a psychotherapist, a doctor who's written a best-selling book, *Driven: Compulsion and Obsession in Everyday Life.* She's still young, in her mid-thirties, probably; chainsmokes unfiltered Camels; can't relax; hardly eats; is consumed by her work, her patients, her writing; sleeps on her livingroom couch instead of in her bed. Despite suggestions intended for her benefit by an older female colleague, Crouse continues her hell-bent regimen. In fact, if this had been a Gold Medal paperback novel of the 1950s, it might easily have been titled *Hell-Bent.*

Bent it is. One of Crouse's patients, a young compulsive gambler named Billy Hahn, confesses to her that he owes $25,000 he doesn't have to some heavy who'll kill him unless Billy can come up with the cash. If the good doctor is so committed to helping him, Billy tells Crouse, why doesn't she do something about that? Crouse takes the bait and goes down to a seedy joint called the House of Games. There are several wonderful shots here reminiscent of Edward Hopper paintings: two of the slightly out-of-focus bartender reading a paper, another of a group of desultory pool shooters. The movie is cast in a dull, muted light throughout, which helps to *verify* the sinister doings. Crouse convinces the bartender to produce Mike, the guy who's holding Billy's marker. Mike, played by Joe Mantegna, comes out of a backroom poker game and confronts Crouse. She tells him to lay off Billy, that he's sick, he needs help and can't possibly pay the twenty-five large he owes. Mantegna produces the paper and shows Crouse that Billy's down for 800 bucks, no more. But look, Mantegna says, if she'll help him out in the poker game, figure if a certain guy is bluffing or not on a big hand, Mantegna will let Billy off for the 800. She agrees to the deal, does her part, but the plan backfires and the scene turns ugly. She winds up almost being fleeced of $6,000 until she sees the whole thing is a con. That's what Mantegna and his pals are, con men; and anyone who enters the House of Games is fair game. It's a big house, too—everyone's in it, but the scams are impersonal; these guys are pros.

Mantegna appears to take a liking to Crouse; he and an avuncular con man cohort, a portly Arthur O'Connell-like character, show her a few minor tricks of the trade. Mantegna hips her to the "tell"—how to recognize the signals people unintentionally send that give away information or their true feelings. It's a clever routine, and Crouse is impressed. She implores Mantegna to show her how he works; she wants to study the game. He takes her along to a Western Union office where he sets up a naive Marine for a fall, but lets him off, leading Crouse to conclude he's really an okay guy underneath the con man cover. That's what hooks her.

Mantegna and the bartender talk with heavy Chicago accents, which is slightly disconcerting to a learned ear, because the movie is set in Seattle. Mamet is from Chicago, and these voices sound authentic to him. Mantegna is magnificent as Mike the grifter, and he sets up Crouse in ingenious fashion for a monster con—or, as he later calls it, a "dinosaur" job, a scam people will one day have to go to a museum to learn about. And Crouse is perfectly convincing as the neurotic mark, Miss Obsessive herself, a tiger ready to jump through the fiery hoop. The tiger, though, gets her revenge; she's the one with the claws, after all, and the reaction is as savage as the con is sophisticated. *She*'s the sicko, not Mike, because she takes everything *personally*.

Mamet's directorial debut is a sharp, surprising crime drama full of parochial lore. The dialogue is presented in a stilted manner that's bothersome at first, but once the information starts flowing and the plot unravels, it seems natural to the moment: formal lessons from Mike, the congenial con shark. The music is integrated subtly, cleverly, never covering for a weak spot, instead supporting a feeling, a shift in mood. Life, this movie would have you believe, is a game the rules of which differ from play to play. And when the deal doesn't go down according to form, there's nothing to do but play past it, go on to the next trick. This is a French-fake of a story, like a rope coiled with each turn wound outside of the other, beginning in the middle. The mark gets her foot caught in the line but she wiggles loose, plays payback, and deals herself a new hand. It's the only way out, otherwise there's nothing lit up on the board but Game Over.

House of Horrors

1946. Directed by Jean Yarbrough. Starring Rondo Hatton, Bill Goodwin, Robert Lowery, Virginia Grey, and Martin Kosleck.

A personal favorite of mine, *House of Horrors* is a fractured exegesis on art, love, and curvature of the spine. The Creeper—

Rondo Hatton—steals the movie, hands down. His hands are usually wrapped tightly around the throat of a prostitute cornered in an alley or on a lonely sidestreet, until he's rescued and taken in by a deranged sculptor who exhorts The Big Guy to strangle an art critic or two.

According to my pal Vinnie Deserio, a plumber *cum* film historian, The Creeper grew up in Tampa, Florida (where Vinnie also grew up and where I happen to be writing this essay), and he had a twin brother. Hatton was apparently a handsome, regular-featured and proportioned fellow until he developed a bone disease that proceeded to disfigure him. He managed to turn this tragic occurrence to his advantage by appearing in a number of movies as The Creeper character or another aberrant, Neanderthal-like rascal. His face really was remarkable: a grotesquely beautiful shape that the sculptor in *House of Horrors* just has to render in clay. A snoopy woman art critic sneaks a peek at the sculptor's horrific work-in-progress, however, and figures out what's up: the serial hooker killer is being hidden out and provided for by the crazy artist who sics his faithful mangler on the critics who have panned his work.

This is all supposed to be happening in New York, but it was obviously shot on a Hollywood backlot on a rockbottom budget. The feel of the movie is genuine, however; there are some seriously scary scenes as The Creeper stalks the streetwalkers. The use of shifting shadows and sudden dark-to-light maneuvers similar to Edgar Ulmer's method in *Detour* are effective tricks that create an appropriately moody black-and-white rhythm. The predictability of the plot and denouement notwithstanding, the real show is The Creeper. *House* is Rondo Hatton's greatest performance; his strange shape and countenance are unlike anything on screen this side of Tod Browning's *Freaks*, or the traveling carny sideshow wagon in Hitchcock's *Saboteur*. The Creeper's problem with women is right on the surface, unquestioned; no hokey psychologizing in this one. Old Rondo's operative philosophy is simple: don't complain, don't explain.

Hollywood's exploitation of Rondo Hatton is no different than the use of Jayne Mansfield: something for everyone.

House of Strangers

1949. Directed by Joseph L. Mankiewicz. Based on the novel *I'll Never Go There Again* by Jerome Weidman. Starring Edward G. Robinson, Richard Conte, Susan Hayward, Luther Adler, Paul Valentine, Efrem Zimbalist, Jr., and Debra Paget.

Edward G. as the great patriarch is simply stunning. Gino Monetti, owner of a bank in New York's Little Italy, father of three sons, and tyrannical ruler of his family, is arguably Robinson's greatest role. Gino runs his bank as he pleases, dispensing loans at whim, taking exorbitant bites but lending dollars for little or no collateral. His eldest son, Joe (Luther Adler), whines and begs to be more than a clerk in his father's bank, wants more money to satisfy his striver, waspish wife. Gino humiliates him regularly, as he does the big goon son, Pietro (Paul Valentine), whom Gino calls "dumbhead." Max (Richard Conte), a lawyer, is the favorite son, the son most like Gino, the one Gino trusts. Joe is envious of Max, of Max's smooth good looks and way with women, and, of course, his princely position insofar as their father is concerned.

When Gino takes a fall and loses control of his bank for violating loan regulations, Max does the time in prison, protecting his father. He does seven years, and when he comes out Joe is running the bank. The old man, who for so many years completely dominated his wife and sons, who insisted on blasting Rossini on the phonograph while they ate—much to the displeasure of Joe and his wife—finally dies, and Joe begins to extract his revenge. He's afraid of Max, though, and his own paranoia and greed eventually do him in. Max's loyalty and stand-up attitude pull him through.

The cleverest parts are reserved for Max's relationship with Irene (Susan Hayward), a rich woman, non-Italian, for whom

Max forsakes his beautiful young fiancée. Irene tries to buy Max, to get him to help her in his capacity as an attorney, but he turns the tables on her and she falls for him. The family crumbles, and Max can give up the rigors of carrying on in the Italian tradition more easily. Irene probably isn't even Catholic! Max is the one who moves into modern society, adopts the fast life, but with old-country values held firm. The old man may have been a monster but he was sharp enough to figure the moves. Hayward is a wastrel, unsure of the direction of her life until she meets Max. He takes over. He gets her and gets the bank, too, along with the loyalty of the big dummy Pietro. To his father Pietro was a palooka, good for nothing but being a guard at the bank and a bad club fighter; to his older brother Joe he could only be a strongarm go-fer; but to Max he's a human being.

Conte played heroes differently than most leading men; in fact, Conte never really qualified as a leading man. He was resentful that Brando got the Godfather role over him from Coppola; but Coppola knew what he was doing; Conte's psychic scar showed on his face and ran right down the middle. Harvey Keitel has the same scar; he's the closest thing to Conte in the movies nowadays. Even as hero Conte couldn't claim innocence or naïveté. Everyone is in his or her right place in the story of The Fall of the House of Monetti. My Uncle Les's fishing buddy Tony Grimaldi, who ran the Columbia Bank in Ybor City in Tampa, was a lot like Gino Monetti; he was tough but fair in his own way. He used to separate people into those who were "on the up and up" and those who weren't, which is relative, I know, but better than right or wrong.

I Died a Thousand Times (See *High Sierra*)

I Walked with a Zombie

1943. Directed by Jacques Tourneur. Produced by Val Lewton. Starring Frances Dee and Tom Conway.

Cat People

1942. Directed by Jacques Tourneur. Produced by Val Lewton. Starring Simone Simon, Kent Smith, and Tom Conway.

The Leopard Man

1943. Directed by Jacques Tourneur. Produced by Val Lewton. Based on a story by Cornell Woolrich. Starring Dennis O'Keefe, Margo, and Isabel Jewell.

I Walked with a Zombie is the voodoo version of *Jane Eyre*. British novelist Jean Rhys had a go at it, too, in her novel *Wide Sargasso Sea*. Without a doubt, one of the eeriest movies ever made. Frances Dee as a nurse who comes to a Caribbean island to attend Tom Conway's close-to-catatonic wife. Conway and Dee go for each other, but they're prevented from consummation by the somnambulist *esposa*. The scene where Dee gets trapped at a voodoo session in the woods will creep out the most intrepid viewers; and there's a zombie chase scene equaled only in the 1940 Bob Hope movie *Ghost Breakers*. Lewton, Tourneur, and Robert Wise made a series of low-budget horror films that remain truly suspenseful and visually exciting: *Zombie, Cat People, The Seventh Victim, The Leopard Man,* and *The Body Snatcher* are the best of them. The light is always hazy, the black not quite black but with an opaqueness that makes you strain to see more clearly. The effect is like looking through a keyhole and being shocked by a cold fingertip on your neck.

Cat People is a masterful understatement of the power of exotic young women over older, rather straightlaced men. Simone Simon, a refugee from mysterious Eastern Europe, holds more than a kittenish attraction for architect Kent Smith, whom she marries but doesn't sleep with. She fears that if her innermost emotions are released she'll turn into a black panther. There's a chilling scene in the restaurant on the night of her marriage where a decidedly catlike woman purrs to Simon "Mya sestrah, mya sestrah," recognizing in her a blood connection more anthropomorphic and feral than spiritual. Kent takes up with a lady colleague since he's not getting any—dare I say it?—pussy from his wife, and Simon stalks the woman, terrorizing her in a basement swimming pool and ripping the lady's robe to shreds.

So much is unexplained in this movie that it works—it's simple but bizarre and very dark. White curls into brown-black. Conway is a duplicitous psychiatrist who tries to get Simon and gets more than he expected. A real wildcat, this foreign number. Remade without any of the subtleties by Paul Schrader with Nastassia Kinski, who transmogrifies magnificently.

Like *Cat People, The Leopard Man*, a shadow-drama set in New Mexico, depends heavily on anthropomorphic suggestion. A few scenes, such as one where the young virgin sits alone at night in a cemetery waiting for her lover-to-be while an escaped black circus leopard prowls the grounds, compare favorably to the earlier cat epic, but the real thrills in this are in the mystery. It's actually a good whodunit and the results are not entirely academic. (That's a joke, as you'll see.)

The Penitente Parade at the end is as weird a procession as anything ever filmed. Lewton and Tourneur knew precisely how to make the innocent and obvious seem strange and unknown. Submitting yourself to them is like giving yourself over to a leering hypnotist and his hunchbacked dwarf assistant named Arg.

I Want To Live!

1958. Directed by Robert Wise. Starring Susan Hayward, Virginia Vincent, Simon Oakland, and Theodore Bikel.

Susan Hayward won an Oscar for her portrayal of party girl Barbara Graham in this one. Graham was a fairly small-time grifter who did what she could for a buck, including prostitution and aiding her boyfriends in robberies and various hustles. She went to the chair for a murder she vehemently denied having committed, claiming she did a lot of things but murder wasn't one of them. Guilty or not, the state of California fried her, leaving her small child motherless and Susan Hayward the opportunity to tear up the screen in a highly sympathetic performance.

The movie captures the spirit of the 1950s, with Hayward hanging out in bebop nightclubs and sporting it up at wild parties, women wearing strapless dresses and high heels, and driving around in flashy Ford Sunliners—all in vivid black and white with which director Wise was a master. Hayward's always willing—or usually willing—to go along on a scam, to help out the boys, so long as there's no violence involved. But something usually goes wrong, and she winds up in jail more than once or twice. Finally she meets a guy she thinks is O.K. and has a kid; of course she's fooled, the guy is definitely wrong; he beats her and doesn't want the child. Hayward takes off and leaves San Francisco, where she's supposed to be living on parole, and goes back to her old haunts in L.A. Pals there hide her out, and in return for shelter and cash she agrees to assist them in a robbery.

Things go bad, and there's no way she can straighten out her life. Hayward and Wise combine to present Graham as a victim of her own big heart and good-time girl attitude. She's no square and no killer, either, they tell us. Her execution was a raw deal.

The film is actually introduced by the San Francisco *Examiner* reporter, Ed Montgomery, who covered the Graham case, so it has the flavor of a semidocumentary. But Hayward has a field day, parlaying conflicting emotions and the seeming inevitability of her landing in an irretrievably bad spot. She was really at her best in more contemporary roles, this one and as Richard Conte's uptown girlfriend in *House of Strangers* (1949). She reflected perfectly the glamorous but shaky character of a woman in transition, not knowing quite what she's doing or where she's going, behaving alternately tough and vulnerable while retaining the vanities expected of a goodlooking gal. As Barbara Graham, the necessity of another lifetime in order to get it right fits the Hayward profile.

If ever there was a woman's movie made in the '50s, this is it. All that's stacked against a woman is in evidence here, and for a chick who's trying hard to be a stand-up guy it's especially gut wrenching. Bodies and shadows pass through, the blacks and whites licking at one another like flames, giving out auras of blue, yellow, green, and gray—until she goes down for the count and everything fades to basic black.

In a Lonely Place

1950. Directed by Nicholas Ray. Based on the novel by Dorothy B. Hughes. Starring Humphrey Bogart, Gloria Grahame, Frank Lovejoy, Art Smith, Carl Benton Reid, Jeff Donnell, Ruth Gillette, and Robert Warwick.

This is an important movie in many ways. As a Hollywood story it rivals Horace McCoy's novel, *I Should Have Stayed Home,* for pure L.A. *angst.* That book, by the way, is probably the best Hollywood dream-factory novel ever written, better than West's *Day of the Locust,* or certainly Fitzgerald's *The Last Tycoon;* and different and more honest than Schulberg's *What Makes Sammy Run?* A shame it's out of print. Anyhow, Nick Ray's ability to present case histories of men and women unable to integrate themselves or remain sane in so-called civilized society is *non pareil,* and *In a Lonely Place* is a masterful study of man's inhumanity to himself, among others.

Bogart plays a screenwriter who hasn't had a hit movie for a few years, largely because he refuses to work on projects he has no feel for. He doesn't respect the producers who beg him for scripts, but he has a faithful agent, played with great sincerity by Art Smith, who keeps after him to work on a movie. Bogey's problem is that he can be a mean drunk even when he's not drinking; he has a violent temper, a raging superiority complex, and is basically a misanthrope. He often doesn't answer the phone when it rings, sleeps late, gets into fights frequently: an adult problem child with talent not unlike James Dean's Jim Stark character as shaped by Ray in 1955's *Rebel Without a Cause.* Bogey is lonely on purpose, but he craves female companionship, and does have real sympathy and affection for the old alcoholic actor played by Robert Warwick, for whom Bogey is always a soft touch. But other than his agent and the washed-up "thespian," as he calls Warwick, Bogey has no friends. One other exception is his old army pal, Frank Lovejoy, who's now a cop on the Beverly Hills force. When a hatcheck girl Bogey's taken home but dismissed early turns up dead, Bogey is murder suspect number one, but Lovejoy defends him to his captain, insisting that Bogey couldn't have killed her.

Enter Gloria Grahame, a neighbor of Bogey's who's had her eye on him. "I like his face," she tells the police captain as she relates how she saw the girl leave Bogey's apartment alone. Bogey seems in the clear on the murder, but the captain is disturbed by Bogey's record of violent outbursts, frequent arrests for assault, and disturbing the peace; he thinks Bogey did it despite what Lovejoy says. Grahame and Bogey fall in love and he begins working on a new script, staying at it day and night and seeming to come out of his prolonged malaise. He's not drinking or fighting for a while and asks Grahame to marry him. But following an irrational show of temper and assault of a college kid over a minor traffic accident (that was Bogey's fault, though he won't admit it) Grahame gets scared; she thinks that maybe Bogey did murder the hatcheck girl after all. Of course she can't confront him with this fear because she thinks he might turn on her; and, of course, that happens anyway. It turns out that he's innocent, that the girl's milquetoast boyfriend murdered her in a jealous rage, but it's too late now for Bogey and Grahame. When he finds her about to skip town on him on the day of their engagement, he flies into a blind fit and starts strangling her. Bogey's brought out of it by the telephone call from the cops clearing him, but he's blown the scene with Gloria. His script is a success, he's back on top professionally, but his life is shot. Grahame gave him something to really live for and now that the opportunity is shattered Bogey is absolutely, irrevocably alone, without much chance that he'll even try for any kind of happiness again.

And that's how the movie ends, on as down a note as possible, except that at least Bogey is innocent of the killing. Visually the movie is often shakily angled (Burnett Guffey was the director of photography), and the road shots are calculated to give the viewer the sensation that he is in the madly careening automobile. Everything is directed toward a feeling of hopelessness; even the friendliness exhibited toward Bogey by Bogey's agent, by Lovejoy and his wife Jeff Donnell, by the restaurant owner Paul, is made pathetic by his intransigence. If ever there was a case of someone being his own worst enemy, this is it, and Nick Ray captured it perfectly. The dialogue is waspish and witty, and Gloria Grahame has perhaps her best role—at least she's not the cheap slut she was usually cast as—and Bogey's disturbed screenwriter presages his Captain Queeg performance. He had a way of frowning that was almost comic, an expression more of confusion than distaste.

This is an unsensationally depicted indictment of Hollywood, in sharp contrast to, say, Robert Aldrich's more hysterical treatment (*The Big Knife,* 1955). It's very ugly, really. Bogey's "likable" face gets plenty unlikable in a hurry.

In Cold Blood

1967. Directed by Richard Brooks, who also wrote the script. Based on the book by Truman Capote. Starring Robert Blake, Scott Wilson, Paul Stewart, John Forsyth, Jeff Corey, and Gerald O'Loughlin. Black and white photography by Conrad Hall.

Truman Capote's involvement with the killers of the Clutter family of Garden City, Kansas—Perry Smith and Dick Hickock—has been well-documented. The multiple murder case and the trial of Smith and Hickock attracted journalists from all over the world. The book Capote wrote was hailed as his greatest achievement, whether it was considered as nonfiction or as a "nonfiction novel"—his own preference. The book was a brilliant portrayal, in the form of character studies, of the two killers and their victims, as well as the principals involved in solving the crime. Capote also captured with Gothic precision the landscape of this part of Kansas. Director Brooks uses a semidocumentary style (not unlike that of Henry Hathaway's *Call Northside 777*) to tell the story, and it works.

The bleak, black and white country—the land—becomes a prime character, more than just another element: a lonesome, cloudy, dangerous presence, as responsible as anything or anyone for what happens. This use of the landscape is as important to the movie as John Ford's or Terrence Malick's. The dark quality of remote flatlands haunts the frame, even indoors. What's outside is real, ominous, waiting; as dramatic and dynamic as a madman in a hockey mask holding a hatchet. Robert Blake has his greatest role here, and his Perry Smith is perfectly complex: the gentle, sensitive, poetic soul who is capable of committing grotesque homicides such as these. Blake takes on Smith's persona leaving no loose ends, no dropped threads. He's an American phenomenon, useful to the French for their peculiar take on the culture, a walking terror with a small-town smile on his face. Scott Wilson is appropriate as the less-sympathetic Hickock, seemingly the "crazier" of the two, the mean one. But in reality it's Smith who pulls the trigger, not Hickock.

Smith and Hickock, fresh from prison, hit the Clutter farm in order to rob the farmer of $10,000 cash he supposedly keeps in his safe. Hickock gets this information from a former cellmate, and it turns out to be unreliable. Once at the house the two systematically slaughter the Clutters: a husband and wife and their children. They split up and manage to avoid the law until the ex-cellmate reads about the crime and comes forward, hipping the warden to Hickock. Life is an impossible situation for these guys; they're multiple losers. Smith is obsessed by the memory of his mother, a former Indian rodeo queen, and is plagued by his short stature, and pains in his legs that cause him to munch aspirin like candy. Hickock is a wicked, country-boy psycho. The pair are like a hillbilly version of Leopold and Loeb.

The movie is full of subtle tensions that eventually explode in sudden violence. The killers are scars on the plain face of the land, scuttling across it like crabs miles from sand, no place to bury themselves, to escape the light. When they're hanged their perverse energy oozes out of them like pus from a wound. As valid a portrait of the heart of the country as *It's a Wonderful Life.*

Invaders From Mars

1953. Directed by William Cameron Menzies. Starring Jimmy Hunt, Leif Erickson, Arthur Franz, and Hillary Brooke.

This movie, along with *The Beast from 20,000 Fathoms,* scared me more than any other horror picture I saw as a kid. I was six or seven years old when Jimmy Hunt woke up during a thunder-storm at twenty minutes to five in the morning and saw the lightning flash illuminate a spaceship that settled down into the sand flats beyond the wood rail fence behind his house. He ran and told his parents, Leif Erickson and Hillary Brooke (whom I already knew from her straight-woman roles in Abbott and Cos-tello shows), and they went to check it out, got sucked down into swirling sand holes, reappearing at the house shortly there-after with little metal-sealed scars on the back of their necks.

They've been neurologically altered by the spacemen, and most of Jimmy's little town ends up similarly sucked down and operated on in some mysterious, extraterrestrial fashion. The Mars guys need a new hangout or something and set up their camp below ground. Jimmy has a tough time trying to convince anyone that his mother and father are no longer his mother and father, that they're automatons being controlled by some hid-eous, malevolent force out beneath the dunes behind his house. There's a scene right out of *The Cabinet of Doctor Caligari* when his mother comes to get him at the police station. Shot from the perspective of a little boy, the sergeant's desk looks gigantic, monstrously high, unclimbable; the walls are doubly high and long, as if he's trapped in an endless tunnel. And that happens, too, when Jimmy finally convinces the local army base officers that something's wrong Out There, and together they slip down beneath the ground into a maze of tunnels occupied by giant bug-eyed galoots carrying rayguns.

The Mars mob is controlled by a small octopuslike creature with a giant brain who operates out of a transparent bowl. Jimmy makes his pitch to the brain-gnome, who manipulates his slaves via mental telepathy, but realizes there's no escape; the army is helpless, his own parents are out to kill him, too, or turn him into a zombie. The war begins when the army shells the site; the Martians go bonkers and start blasting their rayguns, and all hell breaks loose as the cave walls collapse. Then Jimmy wakes up. It's all been a nightmare. There are his parents, smiling Hillary and grinning Leif, assuring him that everything's all right; he's just had a bad dream, that's all.

Boy, what a relief! I mean those Martians had googly eyes THAT big. And that squiggly, ugly little brain man, or whatever it was—not a creature to match it until *Alien*. So Jimmy goes back to bed; all is well. And then the thunder rolls, lightning flashes, Jimmy opens his eyes and looks at the clock, twenty to five. Through the wind and rain and lightning Jimmy sees the spaceship coming down.

When my son saw this picture, also at the age of six or seven, it scared him so much that for months he checked the back of my wife's and my neck. Remade in 1986 by Tobe Hooper for no good reason or result.

Invasion of the Body Snatchers

1956. Directed by Don Siegel. Screenplay by Geoffrey Homes (Daniel Mainwaring). Starring Kevin McCarthy, Dana Wynter, King Donovan, Carolyn Jones, and Larry Gates.

This science-fiction *noir* is a crossover masterpiece. Written by the author of *Out of the Past* and directed by the maker of *Charley Varrick*, *The Big Steal*, and numerous other crime classics, it could hardly miss. The remake by Phil Kaufman was unnecessary—not terrible, just not worth the bother; the original is perfection, and why anyone would want to mess with that is beyond me. (Kaufman, by the way, co-directed a strange and wonderful little non-*noir* movie called *Goldstein*, starring Lew Gilbert and Ben Carruthers, made in Chicago in the mid-60s. It's seldom seen these days but well worth the effort if you can find it.)

The idea of aliens from outer space taking over the earth is one that can never lose currency. Human-sized pods, like pea or bean pods, appear everywhere and reproduce within them the physical bodies of earth residents, transplanting alien minds for human. Only Kevin McCarthy, a doctor, manages to escape the takeover of his small California town, and then can only warn others of their—as well as his own—impending doom.

It's easy enough to see this movie as an object lesson: Don't let others do your thinking for you. And it's as relevant today as it was during the McCarthy era and Cold War panic, when it was first made. It's not that they're coming—they're already here, and always have been. Keep your eyes open or you're a goner. In the movie the aliens take over your mind when your body falls asleep. This is one of the most serious, realistic movies ever made. Don't ever forget it.

Island of Lost Souls

1933. Directed by Erle C. Kenton. Based on the novel *The Island of Doctor Moreau* by H. G. Wells. Starring Charles Laughton, Bela Lugosi, Richard Arlen, and Kathleen Burke.

This movie has the eeriest opening of any film I've ever seen. It's all fog and fog shadows. A shipwrecked couple is picked up by a rattletrap freighter in the middle of the ocean and taken to the island where Doctor Moreau is king. The boat is full of animals intended for use in mysterious experimentation performed by the good doctor. Moreau is played to the creepy hilt by Charles Laughton, who camps it up wildly—raised eyebrow, crossed legs, and all of that. He carries a whip, too, and wears jodhpurs. His performance is extremely arch, allowing him to act out his ordinarily suppressed queeny emotions.

Intended by H. G. Wells as an indictment of social conditions, *Island* is transformed by Kenton and Laughton into an outrageous Barnumlike gymkhana, a paean to anthropomorphism. Paean/pain is the right word, too. Laughton/Moreau operates on the animals, attempting to transform them into men. The failures are left to fend for themselves in the woods. Some of them maintain human traits longer and better than others and stay on at the main house as servants, but when they revert too far to their animal selves they're cast out. Read into this all you like but it makes a great movie.

Richard Arlen is seduced by a cat woman. Bela Lugosi is the leader of the rejects, and Laughton is deliriously megalomaniacal. "Are we not men?" intone the beast boys, who finally rebel and overrun the doctor's manse, torturing him as he has tortured them, dragging him kicking his high leather boots to The House of Pain. Remade in the '80s for no good reason, as usual, with Burt Lancaster as Moreau, with Wells's title. Keep away from that one unless you're a masochist.

Kansas City Confidential

1952. Directed by Phil Karlson. Starring Preston Foster, John Payne, Colleen Gray, Donna Drake, Jack Elam, Lee Van Cleef, and Neville Brand.

A good lowdown drama on a par with director Karlson's 1955 exposé docudrama *The Phenix City Story*. But *K.C.* has a more developed story line than *Phenix City*, a more exotic setting (Mexico), and a super *noir* group of actors, especially Brand, Van Cleef, and Elam. The story is pretty slick: three ex-cons, wearing masks to disguise themselves from each other as well as the citizens, pull off an armored car robbery and make their getaway in a truck identical to the one that delivers flowers on a daily basis to a store next to the bank where the hit is made. The three robbers have been brought together by a former K.C. police captain who's blackmailing each of them, and who's been forcibly retired on a small pension. Each mug has made his way separately and each escapes separately, eventually meeting up in Barados, Mexico, an out-of-the-way resort town, to split up the cash.

John Payne is the real delivery truck driver and he gets hauled in as a suspect, but is soon released for lack of evidence. He's treated brutally, however, and goes after the robbers. He finds Jack Elam in Tijuana, and when Elam is killed by Mexican cops, Payne assumes his identity. He's already beaten information out of Elam about the robbers' rendezvous, so he hightails it to Barados on Elam's ticket. There are some heavy shadow shots of Elam and Payne as they cat and mouse it around Tijuana, in a gambling joint and on the seedy streets and in a hotel room. This is top-notch *noir*-ville. Karlson even manages to make the usually happy-faced Payne look sinister. In Barados, Payne encounters the other two thieves, Brand and Van Cleef—evil-looking customers—and Payne passes himself off as Elam. Preston Foster is the former K.C. cop who really wants to show up the K.C. force by turning the robbers in and collecting an insurance reward. Foster is pissed off that he's been mustered out of the police ranks, so he's worked out this elaborate scheme as his revenge. What he didn't count on was Payne running them down.

Foster passes himself off in Barados as a tourist fisherman, familiar with the country from previous holidays spent down there. His daughter, played by Colleen Gray, shows up unexpectedly, however, and she and Payne fall for each other. Van Cleef is appropriately weasel-like as he plays sleazy-squeezy with the local hotel vamp, Donna Drake, who does a great Lupe Velez prickteasing chiquita routine. Neville Brand is his usual pockmarked no-nonsense heavy. When the cops arrive, the two robbers are shot down and Foster buys it, too. Payne doesn't let on to Foster's daughter that Foster was the mastermind, preferring to let her think her father was a hero who helped do in the thugs, giving him a clean slate in K.C.

George Diskant's powdery black and white photography traces the events streakily, making perfect use of the mood, *forcing* eeriness on us; and unrelieved visual distress. In this way Kansas City, Tijuana, and Barados have a uniformity of tone, giving us the bad side of the picture in which everyone already has one foot in the grave.

Key Largo

1948. Directed by John Huston. Based on the play by Maxwell Anderson. Starring Humphrey Bogart, Lauren Bacall, Edward G. Robinson, Claire Trevor, Lionel Barrymore, Thomas Gomez, Harry Lewis, and Jay Silverheels.

"There's a lot of guns out there, but there's only one Johnny Rocco." One of my favorite movie lines, as uttered by Edward G. Robinson in *Key Largo*. Robinson is Johnny Rocco, a has-been gangster recently deported and trying to reclaim his piece of the territory. He's washed up for good, though, and his boys are as out-of-date and pathetic as he is. Their day has passed but Rocco is crazed, frustrated, desperate to make a deal with his old Miami connection, Ziggy, so that "things will be the same again."

Bogey is in Key Largo to see Lionel Barrymore, the wheel-chair-bound father of Bogey's war buddy who died. Bacall is Barrymore's daughter-in-law, living with him at his hotel during hurricane season. Rocco comes in on his yacht from Cuba to meet up with Ziggy, and his gang has taken over the place. Accompanying Rocco is his former moll, the alcoholic chanteuse Gaye Dawn, played tremblingly by Claire Trevor. Rocco is disgusted by her boozehound condition, and humiliates her in front of everyone by making her sing her old standby, "Moanin' Low," before he'll give her a drink. Disappointed by her off-key, inept attempt at the song, Rocco refuses to give her booze.

Two local Indians, the Osceola brothers—one played by Jay "Tonto" Silverheels—have escaped from the local jail, and the sheriff's deputy comes by the hotel looking for them. Rocco's thugs kill him and hold Bogey and others captive. Robinson is the show, bathing in a tub with a fan blowing on him, giant cigar stuck in a corner of his craw. He terrorizes, bullies, and attempts to charm everyone, including his cohorts. Rocco's a lost soul, a man without a home, a long-gone big shot who won't ever get the world back the way he wants it. He's finished, drowning, and fighting for air. Trevor, too, is absolutely convincing: a shadow-creature struggling to survive the abuse heaped upon her by the world.

A hurricane hits the key, and Rocco refuses to alow the local Indians to take refuge in the hotel, a common practice of Barrymore's during storm season. Rocco himself is driven even nuttier by the wind and rain; it's as if the gods have conspired against him along with the United States government. When the sky clears Rocco commandeers a boat and forces Bogey to run it, Rocco's yacht having been taken by the captain so it wouldn't be wrecked on the rocks during the storm.

Bogey knows Rocco will kill him at some point and Trevor steals a gun and secretly slips it to Bogey. She's left behind and pretends to be distressed by Rocco's abandonment of her. The sheriff shows up at the hotel and discovers his dead deputy, believes Rocco's story that the Osceola brothers did it, and he shoots them when he catches them on the property. On the boat Bogey blows away Rocco and his henchmen, though he's wounded in the process, and heads back to Key Largo, to Bacall.

The death of Johnny Rocco was intended to signify the end of an era, and in a way it's true: the days of the old Mustache Petes were over; organized crime moved into the modern world. Robinson's portrayal of the last of the old-time gangsters coincided with the last days of Al Capone, which were also spent in South Florida, and finished off what Edward G. Robinson began with *Little Caesar*. The King is dead! Long live the King!

Key Witness

1960. Directed by Phil Karlson. Starring Jeffrey Hunter, Dennis Hopper, Pat Crowley, Susan Harrison, Joby Baker, Johnny Nash and Corey Allen.

This is an easy one to miss, since it's not often shown even on late-night TV, but any Phil Karlson effort is worth watching (*The Phenix City Story* and *Kansas City Confidential*, especially). *Key Witness* reunites two players from *Rebel Without a Cause*, Hopper and Corey Allen, as hooligans, along with Joby Baker, pop singer Johnny Nash and slinky Susan Harrison. They're a group of gang kids in LA who slash and trash and steal cars. They're drinkers, dopers and beboppers, miserable and stupid received-style hipsters. Cowboy (Dennis Hopper) stabs someone and Square Joe Jeffrey Hunter witnesses it and i.d.'s him for the cops, led by a black detective, which was considered something of a daring move in a Hollywood movie in those days. The punks terrorize Hunter and his wife and kids in an effort to get him to withdraw his testimony, which they succeed at, if only temporarily.

There's some vicious overacting in this movie: Joby Baker is the stylized cool cat, always wigged out and dangling, a semi-psycho who likes guns, nicknamed Magician. Corey Allen— who was unforgettable as Buzz Gunderson, the chicken-run driver who goes over the cliff racing against James Dean in *Rebel*—is an alcoholic who plays the bigot role á la Robert Ryan in *Odds Against Tomorrow*; he's always riding Johnny Nash, the Negro gang member who's really a Good Kid trapped by bad company. The real star of the bunch is Susan Harrison, as Ruby, the skirt-and-sweater slick chick girlfriend of Cowboy, who takes over the gang when Cowboy is popped for the murder. She's got a sly, easy-to-underestimate presence, a physical insinuation that reeks of Mean. Ruby is a Spider-Slut, a blow-job princess who thinks one step ahead, which is about a half-step more than her cohorts are capble of.

Jeffrey Hunter was a too-handsome young actor who wasn't necessarily a *bad* actor, just a piece of furniture to move around. Pat Crowley, who plays his wife here, was much better, the kind of actress who turned up on TV shows like "Perry Mason" or "Twilight Zone" and always gave a convincing performance. Her hysterical fits have some credence in this, whereas Hunter is a cigar store Indian who sweats. The scene where Ruby beats her up in a phone booth in the courthouse is silly—I mean, why can't Crowley fight back?

As usual, from *Rebel* to *Giant* to *Key Witness* to *Easy Rider* to *Blue Velvet,* Dennis Hopper is the perfect kick-in-the-nuts-when-you're-not-looking character. His Cowboy is a narcissistic nut who is already two feet in the ground and clawing at whomever's around in a desperate attempt to drag them into the grave with him. He'll wreck cars, kids, anyone, anything, for kicks or less. His job here is heavy-handed—he's too loud, *too* sick, too obvious, but still effective. Like crackpot baseball player Jimmy Piersall, Hopper always has that searing insane gleam in his eyes.

There's nothing in *Key Witness* we haven't seen before or more perfectly accomplished, but it's a crazy little lob of a movie, a mudball that hits you in the neck while you're running down the alley and you turn around and catch a glimpse of a couple of eight-year-olds dashing into a gangway. Nothing you can do about it that could really matter, so you wipe off the dirt and keep going.

The Killer Is Loose

1956. Directed by Budd Boetticher. Starring Wendell Corey, Joseph Cotten, Rhonda Fleming, and Alan Hale.

Wendell Corey always seemed to play goofy guys in the movies. Wimps, actually, and this role is no exception. Here he's Leon Poole, a bank clerk with thick glasses. His sergeant in the army used to call him "Foggy"—and of course the ex-topkick shows up at Leon's bank the day of an attempted robbery. Leon tries to stop the robbers and gets konked on the head for it, causing the old sarge to say he'll never make fun of Poole again. The trick is that Poole is the inside man on the heist. Joseph Cotten is the detective assigned to the case, and it isn't very long before he figures out that Poole is in on it. There's a shootout at Poole's apartment house and Poole's wife is killed by accident. At the trial Poole is given three concurrent ten-year stretches for robbery, assault, and attempted murder. Before he leaves the courtroom he fixes his foggy stare at Cotten—and Cotten's wife, Rhonda Fleming, who's with him—and swears he'll get even with him. Cotten shrugs it off as Poole is led away, but Rhonda's disturbed.

At first Poole is a difficult prisoner, but then he straightens out and gets transferred from the Big House to an Honor Farm. One day while working in a lettuce field, he breaks off the blade from a hoe, kills a guard truckdriver, and escapes. Poole then murders a farmer, steals his clothes and pickup truck, and heads for the city to get his revenge on Cotten. The word goes out that Poole used to tell his cellmate in the joint that he's after Cotten's wife: a wife for a wife. Cotten makes Fleming stay at a friend's house, knowing Poole will show up sooner or later. But first Poole calls on his former sergeant, old Otto Flanders, whom he shoots while Otto is holding a bottle of milk, splattering blood and milk together over the kitchen wall. Poole is really whacko now, and takes Otto's wife's raincoat, rolls up his pants legs, and heads for Cotten's house. Fleming, meanwhile, decides she should be with her husband at this crucial time, and she winds up being stalked by Poole as she walks to her house. The place is staked out, of course, cops hidden all around, and when she makes a break for the door the cops blast poor Poole. End of story.

This movie really got to me when I first saw it and I was ten years old. Especially the milk bottle shattering and all the pots and pans falling off their hooks when Poole guns down Otto. Also the creepy stalking scene with Corey disguised as a woman as he follows Fleming. It's not a very complicated movie but somehow serious, believable. Corey is clearly a nutcase who really goes off the deep end after Cotten shoots his wife. He's a man who doesn't need anybody else, doesn't want help, and so he's legitimately dangerous. Directed by Budd Boetticher, a veteran of many westerns, who was also a bullfighter (in fact, technical advisor in 1941 to Rouben Mamoulian on *Blood and Sand*). A solid job all around, with perfect flat '50s photography. Nothing poetic, just the straight goods.

The Killers

1946. Directed by Robert Siodmak. Based in part on a short story by Ernest Hemingway. Starring Burt Lancaster, Ava Gardner, Albert Dekker, Edmond O'Brien, Sam Levene, William Conrad, and Charles McGraw.

Probably the best movie version of a Hemingway story, Siodmak covers the literal ground staked out by EH in the first fifteen minutes. McGraw and Conrad are the perfect pair of torpedoes, and they manage to frighten the hell out of a diner owner and a kid in it (Phil Brown as "Nick"—Hem's Nick Adams, his own boyhood persona partly copped from Sherwood Anderson) before doing the job on The Swede. In the short story The Swede is Ole Andreson, an ex-pug; and in the movie it's Burt Lancaster in his first role. The Swede offers no resistance: he knows it's time, life isn't worth living, and they plug him. But why go down so easily? Why the fatalist? You guessed it: betrayed by a woman. Again. Remember that green scarf with the birds or whatever the hell it had on it? The one she used to wear? Especially if she's Ava Gardner at her loveliest. Just enough to make you swoon and die. If you're The Swede, that is. And that's what we're expected to believe.

Actually, *The Killers* really fits the term *noir;* The Swede's attitude, hiding in the shadows, not a good word to say about the world, more than qualifies. The Swede hooks on to a gang of thieves, the leader of which, Dekker, has this lazy-looking dynamite girlfriend played by Ava. The Swede has his eye on her from the get-go. And after the robbery gets screwed up, he grabs the loot and figures to run off with her. It just doesn't work out that way: she ends up back with Dekker and The Swede sits in his narrow room in the small midwestern town waiting for Godot. Told via a series of flashbacks, and following the investigation of an insurance man, Edmond O'Brien, who's trying to figure out why it all happened, director Siodmak manages to create an entire universe out of the snatch of life Hemingway originally presented. It's a great effort and mostly works. It allows us to attach ourselves to O'Brien's coattails and watch him spin himself out of the boring orbit of the insurance business into the world of the hard guy and harder dame, much like James M. Cain's potboilers based on insurance investigations (viz. *Double Indemnity*).

An interesting feature of this kind of action is all the lying that goes on. Almost nobody tells the truth, especially not to themselves. The Swede is disillusioned, sure, but he's stupid, a brute, really, and it's impossible to feel sorry for him. The gangsters are selfish animals, worthless as human beings; and Ava just wants the cash and a respectable front. She's a boring piece of flesh, lusting to sit around the country club drinking daiquiris. The Swede is the dumb romantic, and the hustling insurance weasel O'Brien is the relentless striver, hard to like. The entire movie is one big low blow, one that put The Swede on the canvas for keeps.

The Killing

1956. Directed by Stanley Kubrick. Screenplay by Jim Thompson; based on the novel *Clean Break* by Lionel White. Starring Sterling Hayden, Vince Edwards, Colleen Gray, Marie Windsor, Jay C. Flippen, Timothy Carey, Elisha Cook, Jr., Ted deCorsia, and Joe Sawyer.

The Killing really pulls in all of the sicko elements of *noir* that master novelist Jim Thompson specialized in. It's basically cruelty heaped on top of cruelty; nobody can get it right so nobody gets anything. End of moral, end of story.

Hayden is an ex-con named Johnny Clay who plans a surefire robbery of a racetrack. He hires Timothy Carey to shoot a horse during a race in order to cause confusion and divert people's attention from the robbery. It's another great Carey performance as he leers and grunts and groans out of his permanent death-mask face. Marie Windsor is, as always, the big breasted blonde who falls for the wrong guy. In this case she's married to a milquetoast track betting-window teller, Elisha Cook, Jr., but has a man on the side, to whom she spills the beans about the robbery, and who throws a wrench in the works. The rest of the guys are typical grifters, dummies out for an easy buck who can't get out of their own way.

The heist goes off as planned but when the gang meets to divvy up the take, Marie's boyfriend and his goons come in and attempt to steal it from them. Everybody gets blown away in this one, except for Cook, who limps home and murders the unfaithful Marie for blabbing and cheating on him; and Johnny Clay, who comes in late, takes the cash in an old valise, and tries to get away with it all himself. He's apprehended at the airport, where, in a scene of real beauty, the suitcase topples off a baggage cart, comes apart, and the bills are blown to hell and back by the wind from an airplane's propellers. This is reminiscent of—if not outright stolen from—*Treasure of Sierra Madre*, where the dumb bandits cut the bags of gold dust off the mules and scatter it to the winds, unaware of what they're doing.

Kubrick uses repeated flashbacks to tell the story, an elliptical style calculated to make the viewer pay attention and build the narrative to a crescendo that ultimately breaks in a wave. It works perfectly, and each face is right for the part. Everyone looks so worried and concerned throughout that their features are marred, twisted, bent, screwed up in the physical as well as psychological sense. Robbing and killing can do that to people, and this is acceptable evidence.

King Creole

1958. Directed by Michael Curtiz. Based on Harold Robbins's novel *A Stone for Danny Fisher*. Starring Elvis Presley, Walter Matthau, Carolyn Jones, Dolores Hart, Dean Jagger, and Vic Morrow.

No cracks, please. *King Creole* is a legit piece of work, and one of Elvis's best performances as an actor. Surrounded as he is by solid movie veterans, and directed by the man who made *Mildred Pierce,* among numerous other memorable films, it's not really a surprise. Elvis really could act when given the opportunity: *Flaming Star, Jailhouse Rock,* even *Love Me Tender,* shows his real talent at moments. Those stupid Hawaiian hula-rock epics destroyed him—man and music—for many years.

The movie opens with El leaning over a balcony singing in response to a black woman coming down a French Quarter street in New Orleans, calling "Crawfish! Crawfish!" And there are a few other songs strewn throughout the picture; one underrated little ditty, "Lover Doll," is especially nice. But Elvis is a young guy exploited by a gangster, played by Walter Matthau in one of his better roles as a heavy. Matthau began his acting career by playing bad guys: *The Kentuckian,* with Burt Lancaster, was his first. And he did it very well. Vic Morrow is Elvis's counterpoint, his nemesis, who works for Matthau. Carolyn Jones, thin, dark, and sexy with those Walter Keane giant kid's eyes, is Matthau's moll but she falls for Elvis. He sees something in her, knows she's really a better person than she seems to be, hanging out with scum like Matthau, but his chick is Dolores Hart. Hart, of course, left acting and became a nun. This was after dating Elvis for a while.

"If you're lookin' for trouble," Elvis sings, "then you came to the right place. If you're lookin for trouble, then look right in my face. Because I'm eeeevull, my middle name is misery." Elvis's cellblock dance number in *Jailhouse Rock* is a gem; and his ability to convey hurt, emotional pain, is genuine in *King Creole, Wild in the Country,* and *Kid Galahad. Wild in the Country,* with Tuesday Weld and Hope Lange, comes closest to *King Creole* in terms of Elvis's veracity as an actor. In that one he plays a jailkid who can write, who wants to be the new Thomas Wolfe, and winds up torn between two women, one older, one younger. This was a fairly common theme for Elvis vehicles. In *Creole,* Carolyn Jones has real sympathy as well as lustful feelings for him, and he's a real gentleman. Elvis's ability to portray sullen, rebellious boys who nevertheless are polite and without malice is no mean feat. With some real words to say, an intelligent script, such as Clifford Odets's screenplay for *Wild in the Country* (which he also directed), Presley made something of it. He was a natural performer, interesting to look at, slightly stupid, and emotionally retarded, which helped make his attempts to cover up his vulnerability ingenuous. Hollywood made every mistake with him. In fact, he might have been as good as James Dean, but after 1956 he never had a chance to be alone.

Kiss Me Deadly

1955. Directed by Robert Aldrich. Screenplay by A. I. Bezzerides; adapted from the novel by Mickey Spillane. Starring Ralph Meeker, Albert Dekker, Paul Stewart, Maxine Cooper, Cloris Leachman, and Gaby Rodgers.

This movie has nothing whatsoever to do with the novel of the same name. Aldrich and Bezzerides just took Spillane's title and ran with it. (Bezzerides also wrote *They Drive by Night, On Dangerous Ground, Juke Girl,* and *Thieves' Highway.* Aldrich's other great film is *Vera Cruz.*) Meeker's Mike Hammer doesn't leer at every voluptuous dame, and he's not an old-fashioned guy. Quite the opposite, in fact: he drives a fancy MG, has a modern apartment equipped with gadgets I haven't seen in use even thirty years later, and seems satisfied with his casual romance with Velma, his secretary. This Hammer is kind of an automaton, almost as if he's been body-snatched and is running on remote control—very remote. His eyes are blank. We learn he is capable of feeling physical pain, that he bleeds, burns, that he can be knocked unconscious, but Aldrich presents him as something of a sociopath.

The story involves the theft of atomic material, something nobody in the movie really knows much about, only that it's valuable and the government wants it back. A girl gets beaten to death over it. Another girl goes up in flames with it. It's the McGuffin. What is really happening here is Aldrich's interior vision, translated onto the screen as life barely under control. Camera angles courtesy of Welles *(Mr. Arkadin)* and Joseph Lewis *(Gun Crazy)*. Aldrich strips L.A. of glamor. A naked girl running on a lonely road at night. All we remember is night. And horrifying scenes like the girl being tortured by men in a basement room: we see shoes, trouser cuffs, Hammer passed out on bedsprings. We hear agonizing screams as the men beat the girl, more screaming, *more!* Until she stops. A guy says to wake her up. Another guy says she won't ever wake up again. We see the men's dark pants' legs, the lower part of the girl tied to a chair. We feel the man's disappointment in being deprived of the pleasure of torturing her some more. It's a truly terrifying, ugly scene.

Hammer doesn't know who he's fooling with, or what. He keeps going back to a mysterious house, coming up the long, curving stairway. A frightened girl in a brown room. Hammer is gray, dark gray, confused, looking for the light. No sun except what's packed down in the lead-lined box, the portable temple of doom.

Kiss Me Deadly is one of the greatest American movies ever made, also one of the scariest. It was a favorite of Truffaut's, who championed Aldrich. Best seen at three A.M. Black and white, mostly black.

Kiss of Death

1947. Directed by Henry Hathaway. Starring Victor Mature, Richard Widmark, Colleen Gray, and Brian Donlevy.

Despite the intermittent, unnecessary narration by Colleen Gray, *Kiss of Death* works cleanly, without a stumble. It's Mature's best acting job. After this his film wardrobe consisted mainly of sandals and a loincloth (viz. *The Robe, Demetrius and the Gladiators,* etc.) And of course *Kiss* was Widmark's most memorable role: Tommy Udo, the psychopathic killer with the most fearsome inferiority complex this side of Mr. Peepers. "Big man, big man," he sneers at everyone, especially Mature. In Udo's universe one is either a big man or a squirt. His best scene is when he pushes Mildred Dunnock down a flight of stairs in her wheelchair.

As thoroughly loathsome as Widmark is as Tommy Udo, Mature's Nick Bianco, an honorable crook forced for his family's sake to turn stool pigeon, is conveniently likable. Mature's droopy eyelids and heavy, dark Sicilian looks place him as the cinematic father of Sylvester Stallone—though Stallone's celluloid mother would have to be Leo Gorcey. Mature fills up the screen while Widmark wriggles sideways into the frame, a nasty little reptile. In order to spring himself from stir Mature pretends to befriend Udo, skillfully pumping him for info on various crimes, carrying it to Assistant D.A. Louie D'Angelo, played by Brian Donlevy. Donlevy, in a rare sympathetic role, feels sorry for Mature, whose wife committed suicide and whose two little girls were stashed in an orphanage. Even the Sing Sing guards like Bianco: "He's not a bad guy," one of them tells the warden. The warden gives Bianco a break, putting him on the prison ball team. "He's got nice handwriting," the top cop comments.

This is a movie of heavy contrasts, incorporating the work ethic, Catholic morality, good bad guy versus bad guy, the corrupt mob lawyer and the decent district attorney. It's also full of excuses—it's preachy and turns nauseating when Mature marries his kids' former babysitter and goes to work in a brickyard rather than fall back to being a grifter. But Nick Bianco confronts Tommy Udo. Coppola probably based the scene in *The Godfather* where Michael Corleone shoots the crooked police captain on this. Udo's a three time loser and Bianco sets him up so the cops can nab him, gun in hand, allowing them to put him away for life. Udo falls for it because he's so filled with hatred for Bianco. He wounds Bianco but gets shot himself, falling in the slick street where he's captured. He who kisses death gets kissed back.

A few years ago I cut out of the newspaper a bizarre little

headline: "Hornets Rout Victor Mature." That's better than Tommy Udo could do.

Knock on Any Door

1949. Directed by Nicholas Ray. Based on the novel by Willard Motley. Starring John Derek, Humphrey Bogart, George Macready, Allene Roberts, Susan Perry, Mickey Knox, and Dooley Wilson.

Other than *Casablanca*, I think this is the only movie in which Dooley Wilson appeared. I might be wrong. Anyway, my guess is that the piano he used in *Knock On Any Door* was larger than the kid-size instrument he played in *Casablanca*. I saw the *Casablanca* piano in an exhibit of Hollywood memorabilia at the Cooper Hewitt Museum in New York, and I couldn't believe how tiny it was. Seeing it on film you'd never think it was so small. Just another celluloid illusion.

This movie is pretty straightforward; a lot of good Chicago street scenes: dirty alleyways, bums stumbling and teetering in the icy winds. A punk named Nick Romano, played by John Derek (his first movie role), can't stay clean, but he's helped out by an attorney, Bogey, who grew up in the same slum environment. Derek repays Bogey's efforts by stealing from him, and almost sours the relationship for good; but then Derek finds a nice girl, marries her, and tries to go straight. Willard Motley's novel, and the sequel, *Let No Man Write My Epitaph* (which was also made into a movie, starring James Darren as Nick Romano's son), are sociological tracts, intended to show the effects of a bad environment on the poor people who are trapped in it. Nick Ray does a good job of showing how tough the situation is, but overall the direction seems self-conscious, predictable, unlike most of Ray's films wherein all manner of crazy events take place (viz. *Johnny Guitar, In a Lonely Place*). But this is an important Chicago movie, exhibiting the kind of world James T. Farrell wrote about.

Derek just can't stay out of trouble, and after his pregnant wife commits suicide he goes nuts and gets involved in a robbery during which a cop is killed. He's arrested and Bogey agrees to defend him, believing Derek's claim of innocence. Prosecuting attorney George Macready is the evil guy, attacking Derek as a ruthless killer, a menace to society. Bogey, of course, counters with an impassioned defense, citing the criminal environment, the impossible circumstances a kid like Derek has to contend with growing up. Bogey really believes Derek didn't do it, but under browbeating examination by Macready, Derek breaks down and admits his guilt. This is a real blow to Bogey, and he can do nothing to prevent Derek from being sentenced to die in the electric chair.

John Derek was a wonderful choice to portray Nick Romano; Derek was extremely handsome and innocent-looking. His eyes were very expressive and he just looks like a pure product victimized by his surroundings. How could a kid like this be such a bad apple? It *must* be the fault of society. It's terrible, but if an ugly, Neanderthal type were cast in the same role, the sociological crapola wouldn't work; nobody much would care what happened to a guy like that. Bogey comes off one-dimensionally, as does Macready. Perhaps the most memorable thing about *Knock on Any Door* is the line Derek uses to express his outlook on life: "Live fast, die young, and have a good-looking corpse." This became a very popular expression among teenagers in the 1950s, most of whom didn't know where it came from. It's probabaly on a T-shirt now.

Laura

1944. Directed by Otto Preminger. Based on the novel by Vera Caspary. Starring Dana Andrews, Gene Tierney, Clifton Webb, Vincent Price, Judith Anderson, and Dorothy Adams.

Laura is High Melodrama, enduring *noir.* Actually a better movie on each subsequent viewing, which is something of a surprise, because at first it seems too pat, too elaborately set up.

But what happens is that the individual performances are worth examining more carefully, and under further scrutiny reveal themselves to be masterful characterizations. That Clifton Webb's performance would be marvelous is no real surprise, nor Judith Anderson's, nor even Vincent Price's—his "Mark Cardigan" in 1951's *His Kind of Woman* is something of a reprise of his "Shelby Carpenter" in *Laura*—but Dana Andrews is exceptionally good here, showing a depth of character I'd never have suspected him of being able to convey. Andrews was one of those World War Two era substitute leading men, like Van Johnson; guys who got the job because so few actors were available. The same thing happened in major league baseball, letting a lot of guys who were lifetime minor leaguers get a shot simply because the regulars were off in the war. But Andrews came through admirably in *Laura* as the detective Mark McPherson, who is called in to investigate the murder of beautiful designer Laura Hunt, played convincingly by gorgeous Gene Tierney. This is easily Dana Andrews's best performance. I never much cared for him as an actor; his looks weren't particularly interesting and he always seemed slightly uncomfortable standing up there on the big screen; he looks better on television, actually. Anyway, he worked out okay in this one.

Rouben Mamoulian was the original director on *Laura*, but Preminger stepped in and made his reputation. His other really good movie is *Anatomy of a Murder*. He concentrates on Andrews, as he should, and watches him fall in love with the portrait of the supposedly murdered Laura. Andrews is a phony hard guy who responds to questions monosyllabically. When Webb asks him if any woman ever really got to him, he says, "A doll in Washington Heights got a fox fur out of me once." So Andrews goes through all of Laura's personal effects, camps out in her apartment, and creepily falls in love with her. He suspects the out-of-pocket playboy Price and the arch, finicky radio personality Webb, but when Laura shows up, not dead after all, she becomes a suspect, too, in the murder of another girl whose face was blown off by a shotgun blast. It gets complicated here, but the story, while intriguing, falls second in interest to the individual performances.

Price is campy and weird as the Southern swain, romancing an older woman (Anderson) who's rich; Laura, who's young, beautiful, and rich, and Ann Redfern, a young model, who's really dead instead of Laura. Webb camps it up, too, but with a panache and carriage that is *non pareil*. He did the same act in *The Razor's Edge* (1946), and to a lesser extent in the "Mr. Belvedere" series. But nowhere was he so forthright with gay mannerisms and speech. Price, too, follows along in this fashion, and the two of them are great bitches, clawing at each other verbally—and all in combat over a woman! *Quel* camp! Cat fights aside, the action is paced perfectly; and Dorothy Adams as Bessie, Laura's maid, is exquisite in her hysterical defense of her employer. (A suggestion of lesbian love? This movie drips with backhanded unconventional sexual innuendo.) Judith Anderson is mostly wasted as the older rich dame attempting to compete for Vincent Price's affections with Laura; she doesn't get enough to do. But any cavils with this picture are minor. It's one of the most cleverly constructed films ever made.

The Leopard Man (See *I Walked with a Zombie*)

The Lusty Men

1952. Directed by Nicholas Ray. Screenplay by Horace McCoy, with David Dortort, and Claude Stamush. Starring Robert Mitchum, Arthur Kennedy, Susan Hayward, and Arthur Hunnicutt.

I suppose the real reason for including this movie is because of my absolute admiration for Nicholas Ray. It's interesting to me that the *Cahiers* crowd of the 1950s preferred Ray over John Huston, partially because they felt Ray was a more naturalistic director and that Huston was an establishment figure, a studio man. I'm sure there were other reasons, but one of the most obvious differences between the two is that more unpredictable things happen in Ray's movies; both directors have made great films, but Ray's have an element of being on the verge of losing control that seduces me in a way that Huston's don't. Huston's masterpiece is *Treasure of the Sierra Madre*, largely because there are no women in it; that's Huston's kind of picture. Ray is definitely more open in structure, malleable, friendly-crazy. I don't get that from Huston.

The Lusty Men is still the best rodeo movie ever made. Sam Peckinpah's *Junior Bonner* is a joke, made especially hokey by the casting of Robert Preston as Steve McQueen's father so that it becomes *The Music Man at the Nampa Stampede*. Cliff Robertson's *J. W. Coop* makes an honest attempt at the field and almost works, but it's a bit stiff and overly stoic. *The Lusty Men* is perfectly low-key, with Mitchum as a former rodeo star who can't compete any longer due to injury and a bad heart. He immediately earns our sympathy because of his unhurried, decent, humble demeanor. Arthur Kennedy plays a neophyte cowboy married to Susan Hayward. He works on a ranch where he gets Mitchum a job and wants Mitchum to tutor him. Hayward, of course, doesn't want her man to get so caught up in the world of rodeo that he can't make a decent living and have a nice, quiet home life. She distrusts and is afraid of Mitchum, despite his assurances to them that he's not the one pushing her husband; it's Kennedy who's pushing Mitchum. There's also the sexual dynamic: Mitchum is the ruggedly handsome, sleepy-eyed object of all the rodeo gals' attention, and certainly Hayward catches this. You half expect them to get together but it doesn't even really come close. She wants a straight act, and Mitchum's too much of a man to cut in on his friend Kennedy's wife anyway. Other than *The Red Pony*, this is perhaps Mitchum's most decent, vulnerable role.

Kennedy gets on the rodeo circuit and he, Mitchum, and Hayward bang their way around. Before all this, however, Mitchum goes back to his boyhood home—a rundown little rancho in Texas—crawls under the house and finds a toy six-shooter he left there when he was a kid. His folks are dead now, and an old man Mitchum doesn't know owns the place. The old man, thinking Mitchum is a thief or worse, points a rifle at him and Mitchum raises his hands and shows the old guy the toy gun as he explains the situation. This is an extremely delicate, tender moment, wistful but not sentimental. It's good evidence of Nicholas Ray's gift, a genuine one.

The Mean Season

1985. Directed by Philip Borsos. Based on the novel *In the Heat of the Summer* by John Katzenbach. Starring Kurt Russell, Richard Jordan, Richard Masur, Joe Pantoliano, and Mariel Hemingway.

The Friends of Eddie Coyle

1973. Directed by Peter Yates. Based on the novel by George V. Higgins. Starring Robert Mitchum, Peter Boyle, Alex Rocco, and Richard Jordan.

A Flash of Green

1985. Directed by Victor Nuñez. Based on the novel by John D. MacDonald. Starring Ed Harris, Blair Brown, and Richard Jordan.

Of these three films *Mean Season* and *Eddie Coyle* embody elements of *noir* attitudes while *Flash of Green* has at its core something more akin to the indefatigability of the human spirit. *Coyle* and *Green* are much better movies than *Mean Season*, but the point of this essay is to pay special attention to the actor Richard Jordan, who appears in each of them. Kurt Russell, Robert Mitchum (who is brilliantly low-key as the hoodlum Eddie Coyle), and Ed Harris are the male leads in the movies but Jordan's performances are so good, while maintaining their complementary status, that something needs to be said.

In *Eddie Coyle,* Jordan was young and goodlooking (he appeared, also with Mitchum, around the same time in *The Yakuza*, a wonderful thriller about the Japanese underworld), and here he plays a kind of dumb Boston Treasury Agent, a Fed doomed by his small-time mind. He squeezed himself down into this one, appearing shallow and hopeless with nothing going on in his eyes other than the one-and-half ideas that would put him under without getting a crack at any real kind of life. By the mid-eighties, Jordan gained an enormous amount of weight and used it to lend real menace to his roles as villain. In *Green* he's a duplicitous, politically ambitious real-estate developer prepared to take out anyone who gets in his way; he's respectable on the surface and reptilian and deadly as hell underneath. As a Florida cracker made good, a good old boy with more on the ball than his cohorts, Jordan's malevolence maintains a vicelike purchase on the screen; his heaviness is a perfect counterpoint to Ed Harris's reedy type of strength.

It's in *The Mean Season,* however, that Jordan absolutely dominates and turns in what is not only a *tour de force* performance but manages to make a mediocre, predictable movie into his own version of The Mad Hatter's tea party. Jordan plays a "numbers" killer, a whacko who contacts Miami newspaper reporter Russell and tells him he's going to murder a certain number of men and women for no obviously apparent reason. Russell is Jordan's conduit to the public, the way he gets attention. The killer is much smarter than the reporter, of course, and is even able to fake him out by meeting him without the reporter knowing he's with the killer. This scene, with Jordan pretending to be a crippled Vietnam veteran living in a trailer park, reminded me of Sherlock Holmes disguising himself so successfully that even (and especially!) Dr. Watson didn't know who it was. Jordan's voice reflects the insanity of the character with perfect creepiness, informing it in such a way that nothing but a monster could be on that end of the receiver.

My guess is that Jordan made a real study of Robert Mitchum. Many of his mannerisms, a deceptive, false lethargy, and now a ponderousness, increasing the feeling of malign desperation, are derivative. Mitchum's Max Cady in *Cape Fear* and crazed preacher in *Night of the Hunter* are inspiring models for Jordan's likewise deranged characterizations. Jordan uses all of himself: he can look, sound, move to fit the role. A great actor.

Mean Streets

1973. Directed by Martin Scorsese. Starring Harvey Keitel, Robert DeNiro, Amy Robinson, and Cesare Danova.

This was Scorsese's first great movie. It built on his first feature-length film, *Who's That Knocking at my Door?*, wherein Harvey Keitel played a hardcase city animal who goes out to the suburban countryside and finds himself lost. A friend of mine from the old neighborhood once accompanied me on a trip from Chicago to Ann Arbor, Michigan, and back; when we hit the Chicago city limits on our return he shouted, "Civilization at last!" That's pretty much the theme of *Knocking*, a not very well-developed black and white film that led to *Mean Streets*, which is as coherent, tough-minded and well-directed a movie as any I've ever seen.

Harvey Keitel and Robert DeNiro are boyhood pals now grown to young manhood. Keitel is the nephew of the local mafia chief in their Little Italy, New York, neighborhood. DeNiro is the nutty Johnny Boy, an irresponsible, immature but loveable—to Keitel—guy, who manages to get in serious Dutch by borrowing money from the loan sharks and not repaying it on time. He looks to Keitel to keep him from getting squashed, and Keitel does his best, which eventually is not good enough. There are a multitude of brilliant scenes and situations here: the colorful Feast of St. Anthony; a welcome home party for a neighborhood buddy just back from Vietnam that turns nasty; a fratricide in the guys' bar hangout; the bar owner showing some of the guys his pet tiger and cooing lines from William Blake as he caresses it; and a bloody shootout finale.

Keitel's constant battle with his Catholicism, his deep sense of guilt about practically everything he does, is rendered in marvelous detail, down to his fascination with self-abuse, burning his fingers in a candle flame. He's having an affair with his cousin who is an epileptic, and he has to keep it a secret because they're close relatives. His loyalty to the crazy Johnny Boy keeps getting in the way of his own life, and his girlfriend/cousin, Amy Robinson, keeps nagging at him to abandon Johnny Boy, cut him loose—in fact, cut out of the whole neighborhood scene and start a new life with her somewhere else. But the neighborhood—Mott Street, Mulberry Street, Elizabeth Street—lower New York—is his universe, the only turf he cares about or understands. There's a lovely interlude where he and his cousin are walking along the beach after one of their secret trysts in a hotel, and Keitel, dressed in dark raincoat and sunglasses, tells her that he hates the sun, the water, the sand. He likes the streets, the concrete, cars with tinted windows, linguini with clam sauce; her dream of escaping Little Italy with him is just that, a dream. No chance.

Scorsese's use of music is particularly meaningful and relevant to each movie he makes. In *Mean Streets* he utilizes the sounds of the early 1960s—the girl groups and early Stones—to liven up the proceedings, to back it up and occasionally punch home a scene. This is no small talent, it's important—just like the use of "Cavalleria Rusticana" over the credits to *Raging Bull* a few years later. He really knows how to set the audience up. *Mean Streets* is an American masterpiece and *noir* as they come.

Mildred Pierce

1945. Directed by Michael Curtiz. Based on the novel by James M. Cain. Starring Joan Crawford, Jack Carson, Zachary Scott, Eve Arden, Bruce Bennett, Ann Blyth, Veda Ann Borg, and Butterfly McQueen.

This is a fierce movie; better than the book, which is unwieldy and clunky and uneven. But the material is great stuff, and this is the one that Joan got her Oscar for, deservedly so. You almost have to sympathize with her throughout this 111-minute soaper. Joan and her husband Bruce Bennett have a difficult time: one of their daughters dies (the good one), and the other, Ann Blyth, turns into the most dedicated bitch Cain could create. Of course, it's basically the same bitch he made in *The Butterfly* (made into a terrible movie with Pia Zadora), and *The Postman Always Rings Twice* (Lana Turner, then Jessica Lange), but Blyth out-bitches the bunch of them.

Bennett fools around with a floozy down the block (this is Southern California in the '40s, all neat little houses in a row), so Joan kicks him out and she gets a job waitressing. She buddies up on the job with Eve Arden, the cashier, who gives her standard marvelously droll performance. Joan works so tirelessly that she starts her own restaurant, Mildred's, hires Eve Arden, and provides daughter Blyth with everything her venal little heart can desire. Zachary Scott steps into the picture as a sneery ne'er-do-well playboy who charms Joan. He lives in Pasadena in a once-great mansion, and that old name and old cash stuff impresses the hell out of a striver like Joan. It also impresses Blyth, who comes on to Scott and outdoes her mother in the romance department. Joan can't see the forest for the trees, as they used to say. She does know that the restaurant is going great guns, and she franchises like crazy. She becomes a wealthy woman. All this time she's fighting off the attentions of obnoxious Jack Carson, her former husband's business partner. Bennett starts to look more and more like a good guy, especially when contrasted to Carson and Scott. Then of course Scott gets murdered and Joan gets to battle it out with the monster she created.

The theme here is greed, like always, except it's Southern California style. We get beach houses, mansions, drive-ins, swanky yellow convertibles, adultery out the wazoo, and prick-teasing at its middle-brow best. We got the sleazy Romeo we know is no good from the get-go, the grasping slit-eyed daughter, the pawing dumbo neighbor; and in their midst is upright Joan, game old Mildred, Miss World Ethic of 1945. Cain knew how America would respond to this slough of confused, unfortunate folks, and it made him a pile of dough. Give a dog a bone and the pack comes howling after him from blocks away. Just like real life. You can smell the blood all the way through this one without having to see it, and that's what makes it so good. Michael Curtiz hustled these players through their paces lickety-split, just like *The Charge of the Light Brigade* a decade or so earlier. They could have called this one *The Charge of the Greed Brigade.* Money to the left of them, money to the right of them, and not a buck to keep. When Joan comes off as the good girl you know you've got wild horses loose in the drawing room and forget about the furniture.

Ministry of Fear

1945. Directed by Fritz Lang. Based on the novel by Graham Greene. Starring Ray Milland, Marjorie Reynolds, Hillary Brooke, Dan Duryea, Carl Esmond, Alan Napier, and Percy Waram.

Of all Graham Greene's books—and there are a great many—my favorites are those he chose to categorize as "entertainments"; his intention was to distinguish them from his more serious novels. Of those "serious" fictions, I think only *The Comedians* is as good as the entertainments, and also the one that could most easily fit into the lighter category. *Ministry of Fear*—an entertainment—is a brilliant little novel, and Fritz Lang made it into a good film. Apparently Lang had wanted to make this movie for some time before he was finally given the opportunity, and it's easy to see why. The story presents a seminal World War Two situation wherein the fate of Europe is contained in a cake.

Ray Milland plays an ex-con in London, recently released after having been imprisoned for a killing he did not commit. He is mistakenly given a prize cake in a church bazaar, a cake containing microfilm that reveals the plans of England's invasion of the Continent, meant to be passed to a Nazi spy. Milland is pursued by the Nazi agents—most terrifyingly by the depraved killer Travers, portrayed by Dan Duryea, who likes to stab people to death with a pair of scissors—and winds up having to bust the espionage ring himself because the coppers think he's a murderer.

There's an eerie white fog Lang concocts as a kind of Chinese screen through which the action is viewed. Sometimes the characters are barely visible—fragments passing across, misplaced images—all of which adds immeasurably to the mysterious activity. There's an Esperanto school, and wheezing oversized ladies in large hats who are really collaborators instead of nice, simple church members. Milland moves through the mist without an anchor, unable to trust anyone, as it turns out, even his wife. And Milland has a wonderful face for this role: he carries a permanent expression of wonderment, fighting to retain a semblance of belief in goodness, in the possibility of goodness in human beings. Is betrayal inevitable? he asks.

As in *The Third Man* (1950), a story Graham Greene wrote especially for the screen for director Carol Reed, *Ministry of Fear* contains virtually no daylight: both stories combine *noir* effects with a World War Two background, a relatively uncommon occurrence. John Huston's *Across the Pacific* (1942), a *Maltese Falcon* cast reunion, and Orson Welles's *Journey Into Fear* (also 1942), are two other *noir* war pictures that are successful. But *Ministry of Fear* is fascinating escape fiction, the highest quality stuff. Beware a blind man in the fog!

Mr. Majestyk

1974. Directed by Richard Fleischer. Based on the novel by Elmore Leonard. Screenplay by Elmore Leonard. Starring Charles Bronson, Al Lettieri, Linda Cristal, and Lee Purcell.

"I just want to get my melons in," Bronson keeps saying in this movie, and after the fourth or fifth time, you've got to believe him. Bronson is a melon farmer who gets involved with some migrant pickers and gets himself arrested and thrown in the local jail. When he and a few other prisoners are being transported in a county jail bus, he's handcuffed to a mob hit man, played by Al Lettieri. The mob tries to bust Lettieri loose and in the confusion and gunfire Bronson takes off, dragging the trigger-german with him. Lettieri, a big-shouldered piece of beef with an Italian fruit-peddler mustache, tells Bronson he'll pay him $25,000 to let him go. But Bronson wants to make a deal with the cops—he'll give them Lettieri if they leave Bronson alone long enough to get his melons in. See, they're rotting out there in the field, and unless he can do the job now, he'll lose the entire crop.

Bronson and Lettieri are like an aging tag team, two actor-wrestlers who keep bitching at one another; though Charlie, of course, is the noble one while Lettieri is the vicious, foul-mouthed brute. Al plays basically the same role he did in *The Getaway*, cruel as Basil Rathbone in *Tower of London* or Laurence Olivier in *Richard III*. (The difference is that neither Rathbone nor Olivier wore an Italian fruit-peddler mustache.) Linda Cristal plays the sultry chicana who picks up Bronson, and Lee Purcell is Lettieri's devoted and delicious gun moll. Bronson doesn't really mind Cristal's attention but life beyond the melon patch isn't quite happening for him. I mean, he can read and write and discuss Aristotelian logic but not today. Today he's gotta get them melons in. Along the way Bronson brushes aside the scuzzhound union breakers, dumb cops, mob executioners, etc. But he cries when the monsters machinegun all the melons gathered in his barn.

Lettieri really is the star here: his bullnecked killer is absolutely, thoroughly believable. The movie gains a curious sort of gracefulness as it progresses, a rhythm almost imperceptible at first, but once you see how action and landscape are wedded, it's easy to watch even with the sound off. In fact, once you've heard Bronson give his spiel about the melons two or three times, it's probably just as well to dispense with the dialogue. This is Elmore Leonard's spaghetti western set in the San Joaquin Valley; actually a *melon* western, maybe the only one of its kind. Determination, Bronson is thy name. If Peckinpah had made it, movie lizards would consider *Mr. Majestyk* a masterpiece.

Night Moves

1975. Directed by Arthur Penn. Starring Gene Hackman, Jennifer Warren, Susan Clark, Edward Binns, and Melanie Griffith.

Gene Hackman is as good an actor as anyone alive. I think I first recognized that fact when I saw him in Coppola's *The Conversation*. His ability to play repressed, incomplete characters, silent sufferers, substituting a confused kind of dignity for forthrightness, for an open expression of feelings, is almost frightening. It's creepy. In *Night Moves* he's a private investigator, former running back for the Oakland Raiders, now living in L.A., who gets hired by a wealthy former movie starlet/slut to find her teenage daughter. The subplot involves Hackman's wife, played by Susan Clark, who's having an affair with a family friend—a sensitive, artistic type who's crippled physically but provides her with an emotional closeness Hackman doesn't seem capable of giving. When Hackman tails them and confronts them, it's *his* failures he's faced with, and there's not much more he can do about it but stick his tail between his legs and shuffle off to the Florida Keys to locate the runaway vixen.

Like mother like daughter. The teenage temptress has slept with or attempted to sleep with every male around, including her stepfather, who's involved in various nefarious businesses in the Keys. His cohort, Jennifer Warren, and Hackman hit it off in a low-key way. She's an ex-hooker, city tough chick. "Down here I'm pretty hot stuff," she tells Gene, meaning there's not much local talent—and she's right. The Florida Keys are not famous for their beautiful females. It ain't L.A. or Palm Beach. Hackman figures out there's something phony going on, a smuggling operation organized out of L.A. by Edward Binns, a movie mogul, but he's reluctant to follow it up; his job is to restore Miss Hot Pants to her drunken tramp mother back on the Left Coast.

But the subtle dynamic here is really between Hackman and Warren. She's a bold presence in the way Penn likes to work his women: Dunaway in *Bonnie and Clyde*, the one girl in the crowd in *Four Friends*. But then he likes to do away with them rather extravagantly: in this one via decapitation by boat. I get the feeling Penn isn't a happy filmmaker at all; he's one idea short in almost everything he does, and so we're left with half gratification. Visually the movie swims along, however. West and East coasts are wedded and we don't skip a beat. This is a mystery but the edges are what captivate us, the raggedy, torn pages of the book.

Everybody's doomed, of course, despite all the L.A. and Florida sunshine, Cubano salsa, Tequila daiquiris, etc. Empty vessels searching for something to fill them up: the teenager and her mother's search for cock to stuff them; the men's struggle for goods, to have something to peddle. This is a sad story, full of pathetic cases. Daylight is just some stage we have to go through to get to the moments of truth. Everyone's behavior is shameful, low-rent. Penn succeeds in not giving us one likable character. If that ain't *noir*, what is?

Night of The Hunter

1955. Directed by Charles Laughton. Screenplay by James Agee from the novel by Davis Grubb. Starring Robert Mitchum, Shelley Winters, and Lillian Gish.

Most notable as Charles Laughton's sole directorial effort, *Night of The Hunter* is superb in every way, particularly for Mitchum's role as a crazed preacher. Mitchum terrorizes a group of kids and old lady Gish in his effort to get at a sack of money. He has "Hate" tattooed on the knuckles of one hand and "Love" tattooed on the knuckles of the other, but it's the devil who's got him impaled on his pitchfork, causing the failed servant of the Lord to murder women and drive himself to the final act of desperation. (Reprised in new guise in *Cape Fear*.) Laughton did a great job directing and it's curious he never tried it again. (The film was a financial failure and that was probably the reason.)

Night has about it the feeling of man's inevitable failure to survive his own hand. A child's nightmare vision of the adult world. No exit.

(A footnote re Miss Gish and another surviving—as of this writing—actress of considerable vintage and prowess: Gish and Miss Bette Davis, reported Hollywood gossip columnist Harry Haun, were not exactly bosom buddies during the filming of *The Whales of August* [1987]. "Once," Haun wrote, "when director Lindsay Anderson complimented Gish"—considered the First Lady of the Silent Screen for her films directed by D. W. Griffith—"on a lovely close-up, Davis snapped from the sidelines, 'Of course it's a lovely close-up! The bitch invented closeups!' ")

Nightmare Alley

1947. Directed by Edmund Goulding. Produced by George Jessel. Starring Tyrone Power, Joan Blondell, Colleen Gray, Mike Mazurki, and Helen Walker.

Had some unknown, or relatively unknown, male actor starred in this movie, rather than Tyrone Power, it wouldn't have made money but it would be revered by *noir* nuts and highfalutin film aficionados everywhere. As it turned out, *Nightmare Alley* didn't turn much of a profit despite Power's presence; the movie-going public of the 1940s didn't like seeing the pretty boy get his fluffy eyebrows soiled in a geek pit. And so what we have is not quite here, but neither is it really over there. It's not bad, though, and worth watching. Personally, I think casting Ty as a carnival lout who becomes a famous mentalist—thanks to the trick he cops from Blondell, hustling her for the bucks—and then sinks into geekdom, was not an altogether bad idea. And he gets a chance to act here rather than brandish a sword or look suave and romantic in a big-shouldered suit.

Ty gets a job with a traveling carnival that has the usual complement of carnival characters: a strongman (played by Mike Mazurki), bearded lady, and so forth; but the act that captivates Ty is Joan Blondell's mentalist routine with her drunken male partner (if I recall correctly, her husband). The guy has sworn Blondell to secrecy about the trick necessary to the act, but of course handsome Ty comes on hard to her, romances her—even though he's out after the young chick, Colleen Gray—and eventually he and Colleen (whom Ty is forced to marry in a shotgun ceremony) kick the carnival and take their act into the big time. They play fancy nightclubs and get to the top. But Ty is a natty little sonofabitch and a womanizer, and we know he's gonna get it back in spades. This is instant karma on the level. He winds up being blackmailed by a shrink, the act goes under, scandal, etc. His only alternative is to go back to the carnival.

Only now Ty is a hopeless alcoholic, like the guy Blondell had in the first place. Ty gets the lowest act going, an act outlawed in most places: he becomes a geek, a phony "wild man" who bites the head off live chickens in a sawdust pit for a bottle of whiskey. It's sick and ugly and the angels are avenged.

The thing about this movie that I like so much is that it makes me remember carnivals like this, the little shows that used to tour the midwest until the 1960s came along and gobbled up all the property the carnivals used to set up on. There used to be a great small carnival with a sideshow that came every year and set up for a week or two across the street from my grammar school in Chicago. The owner used to hire some of us kids to help put up booths and run errands for the workers; and of course we got free passes to the show. About 1961 a funeral home was built on the carnival site and it never came back to the neighborhood. That carny may have had a geek but I never saw him; he may have been in the "adults only" section. A friend and I tried to sneak in there to see the hermaphrodite but we got caught and thrown out.

Northwest Passage

1940. Directed by King Vidor. Based on the novel by Kenneth Roberts. Starring Spencer Tracy, Ruth Hussey, Robert Young, Walter Brennan and Nat Pendleton.

One of my favorite childhood films was *Northwest Passage*, I must have watched it on television (usually at eight-thirty Saturday or Sunday mornings when it wasn't Johnny Mack Brown westerns) a dozen times; stirring jut-jawed Tracy as buckskinned Major Robert Rogers leading his greasy outlaw-wild but brave band of Rangers against the Abenaki and other Northeast tribes.

Of course at that early age I wasn't fully aware of how Rogers' Rangers was really just an expeditionary force for the expanding and exploitative colonies. I saw it precisely as Hollywood wanted it seen, as savage Indians slaughtering innocent New England farmers, families stripped and scalped in the night by sneakfoot Huron or Iroquois. No Indian could be trusted, as shown by the Mohawk scouting party leading Rogers' men into a French gunboat patrol.

Robert Young was cast as a young ex-Harvard student expelled essentially for a romantic nature exercised in his painting and drawing ability, leading Rogers—who discovered Young (as Langdon Towne) with itchy, cantankerous but overly-loyal (the ultimate American saving grace) Walter Brennan, named "Hunk" Marriner, in a country inn, their being on the run from the local British authorities for "revolutionary" activity—to believe Towne could be of use as a map-maker, cartographer, and so shanghais him, with sidekick geezer Brennan, after a substantial intake of ale. Young becomes a Ranger, as such Major Rogers' educated pet, but is shown no favoritism. In the most significant sequence of the film, after Towne-Young is wounded, he is forced to follow at a slower pace, supported by Brennan, naturally, limping in long after the men have made camp—an army can't cater to one man, no matter who or how heroic. It was up to Towne to keep up, and each morning at daybreak—before—Rogers would say, "See you at sundown, Harvard—" and Towne would grimace-smile, holding his side bloodied by a French round, and plucky be-whiskered Walter would squawk, "We'll be there, Major, don't you worry none—just save us some stew!'' Tracy-Rogers would wrinkle his sturdy forehead and nod, turn away.

At one point I even read the book, by Kenneth Roberts, but it was boring compared to viewing the action on the screen, though I liked it. I read a great deal even then, biographies of so-called great men mostly: Clarence Darrow, Jack London, General Custer!, but also Black Hawk, Tecumseh, Osceola—and tried to read another Roberts novel, *Lydia Bailey*, but failed. I'd been ruined by that movie.

Major Rogers' dream, of course, was to find or forge an unknown Northwest Passage, and for that he had to travel across the continent, far from the colonies, and wanted Towne to come with him, chart the route. But Towne's sweetheart was in Boston, or nearby, and Rogers saw his sketches of her—Ruth Hussey—and knew one day Young would prefer to stay behind.

But before that there are some remarkable scenes. Starvation overtakes Rogers' Rangers, forcing them, after a ''successful'' campaign entailing pulling boats over mountains and wiping out an Abenaki settlement in revenge for their apparent brutal ''massacre'' of white family farms, to live on a few handfuls of dried corn a day, led on by Tracy's stern encouragements, endearments, promises of food a-plenty upon reaching the fort where the Redcoats have bearmeat, lamb, deer, roasts galore, imploring them to hold on, stay steady, they'll make it like heroes they already are.

On the way though one man—Crofton—cackles strangely and seems to be holding up okay, but with a mad gleer in his eye. Tracy finally finds him with a secret bundle, the head of an Abenaki Indian wrapped in a blanket he was preparing to eat. Crofton rushes over a cliff flailing at Tracy, and the understanding commander solemnly salutes his fatal plunge. Another Ranger, played by Regis Toomey, breaks his leg so badly he can't—unlike Langdon Towne—carry on, and stays in the swamp with his gun, watching the men march off. One more runs crazy in the hills, ''seeing'' his home, throwing gear aside, doomed.

The rest straggle on, and finally make it, staggering into sight of the fabled fort. Rangers has them straighten up and march like stiff proper soldiers not to show their suffering, but when they get there the fort's abandoned, and they break—until not-too-distant fife and drum apprise them of arriving Redcoats who enter with all Rogers has promised, meats, medals, and outspoken tribute.

When next Rogers and his handpicked horde depart, Towne stands by the picket fence with his babe watching them go with mixed emotions. Tracy stops and poetically details the projected trek to the plains—through Sioux, Arapaho, Cheyenne, "Indians no white man has seen before"—in the hope of discovering the Northwest Passage. Young gulps, wants to go, but he's pussy-whipped. Tracy agrees it's best for him to stay with her, and with the words "See you at sundown, Harvard," walks off after his men, turning at the last to wave once before disappearing over the horizon.

I watched *Northwest Passage* once on television in London, with three South Africans, and they fell asleep about halfway through. Some years after that I went to see it at a special kids' matinee in Berkeley, California, but it was a mistake. The few adults there booed Rogers and his men, cheered the Indians, and, as I slid lower in my seat, hissed their inaccurate portrayal. I had to agree, the movie was distorted, and I left before it was over.

Walking home in the late gray afternoon I recalled what I hadn't stayed to see, to the last scene, whispering Spencer's parting words, "See you at sundown, Harvard"—and gave a final wave.

Odd Man Out

1947. Directed by Carol Reed. Based on the novel by F. L. Green. Starring James Mason, Robert Newton, Dan O'Herlihy, Kathleen Ryan, and Cyril Cusack.

It's Belfast just after the war. The young and sensitive James Mason is the chief of a rebel squad, "The Organisation" they call it instead of the IRA: Johnny McQueen, eight months in prison before he escaped, and since then six months inside a safe house, hiding out. The plan is for Johnny and two others to rob a mill office for funds to support The Organisation. A pretty young woman, Kathleen Ryan, who lives in the house, is all eyes for the trembly Johnny; but he's all for the cause, doesn't respond to her attentions.

The boys don't want Johnny to take on the task of the actual robbery: he's not been out on the streets for too long, but he insists on participating. At the mill they get the loot but Johnny falters on the steps coming out; his eyes blur, he gets dizzy, and winds up being wounded by a guard and killing the man himself. As the getaway car careens around a corner Johnny falls out and has to crawl away on his own, the cops after the car. An all-out manhunt ensues. Long angle shots of wet dirty Irish cobblestone streets. It starts to rain, then snow. Dirty, poor kids begging. Chimney pots smoking. Bleak landscapes out of Bill Brandt. Everybody in this neighborhood is a Dead End Kid.

McQueen manages to get to a raucous giant barroom where the owner hides him in a private locked booth. In the meantime his cronies are turned in by an old bitch who plays both sides of the fence, informing to the cops so they'll let her run her gambling parlor. The other two robbers are shot and killed, the third planner arrested trying to help Johnny. McQueen's badly hurt, bleeding, losing the little energy he had left. The fair Kathleen goes to Father Tom, a sympathetic priest, for aid; and she makes a deal with a tugboat captain at the river to take Johnny out of town that night. A creepy little guy spots Johnny and tells his wild-haired neighbor, Robert Newton, a crazed painter, where he is. Newton lives in an old tumbledown flat with snow flurrying through the roof. He wants to paint Johnny before he dies, to capture the look in his eyes! Newton enters the film about halfway through and steals it straightaway. Kathleen is running all over, searching for Johnny; but Newton, named Lukey, gets him, and installs him in a chair under harsh light while he attempts to render his likeness. Another inhabitant of the building, Tabor, a former medical student, patches up Johnny's wound, but says he must get to the hospital for a transfusion or he'll die. Newton's in a frenzy, wrapped in motheaten tweed coat and long scarf, the snow blowing in, feverishly painting away.

Finally Johnny escapes, making his way with the aid of the creepy pal of Newton's toward Father Tom's church. The cops are everywhere, closing in. They're tracking Kathleen and keeping an eye on Father Tom. McQueen collapses in someone's yard, crawls in the street; the creep runs on ahead to tell Kathleen. She comes to Johnny, helps him toward the harbor where she's convinced the captain to wait until midnight. The clock chimes; the blizzard increases. Kathleen and Johnny are caught against a fence by the river as the cops close in on them, torches bright. Johnny tells her to run, get away. "They'll take us both," she says and pulls a gun, fires twice at the bulls, who fire back, killing Johnny and the faithful daughter of the revolution. Their bodies turn white under the falling snow. The boat goes by on the river. It's the World's End, me boy-o. Work, love, suffer.

Odds Against Tomorrow

1959. Directed by Robert Wise. Adapted from the novel by William McGivern. Starring Robert Ryan, Harry Belafonte, Ed Begley, Gloria Grahame, and Shelley Winters.

A tough, bitter movie superbly rendered by Wise who broke in with the Jacques Tourneur/Val Lewton gang (*The Body Snatcher, The Seventh Victim, Cat People, I Walked with a Zombie, Nightfall*). Wise knew how to string the viewer along—pull him in and play him off—and McGivern's story of a botched hold-up has the perfect tension for him. Robert Ryan as Earl, the southern racist, is brilliant. He keeps his lip curled like Elvis and antagonizes Belafonte to a logical conclusion. Those two with Begley are to rob a small Pennsylvania bank. What we get on the way is one of the great moments in American *noir* when

Ryan comes on to Grahame, his easy mark neighbor: they play, paw, vie for control and finally she says—they're both married, Ryan to the frowsy Winters "Well, just this once." Those famous first words.

Begley tries to keep Harry and Ryan cool, and Harry does *look* cool—he started a new trend in American dress by wearing a heavy turtleneck, sportjacket and shades throughout most of the movie. Though not as pervasive as James Dean's red windbreaker, a lot of guys affected that turtleneck look in the early '60s. Begley's planned the whole thing perfectly, of course. He needs a black man to get them in the back door of the bank at night, to impersonate the colored coffee delivery boy. Ryan has the souped-up old woody for the getaway. But it all blows up—Begley's gunned down, wounded badly, and rather than go to jail again (they're all ex-cons), he shoots himself in the head. Belafonte and Ryan run for it and the cops catch up to them just in time to watch the ending stolen directly from *White Heat.*

Odds is a seedy, unpleasant take on life in America in the late 1950s. Almost as if *It's a Wonderful Life* were going on somewhere in the background, in the same town, with Gloria Grahame as the link between them: the bad girl in the nice little town, and we get a peek at her life on the underside. The French like this one, what with racial hatred, hair-trigger violence, tramp wives, the cool spade in shades, bleak highways, lonesome landscape, wet, dark streets. The U.S.A. at its best. There is a great deal of truth in this one, though, and, as usual, that's hard to take.

On Dangerous Ground

1952. Directed by Nicholas Ray. Screenplay by A. I. Bezzerides and Nicholas Ray. Based on the novel *Mad with Much Heart* by Gerald Butler. Starring Robert Ryan, Ida Lupino, Ward Bond, Ed Begley, Charles Kemper, Anthony Ross, and Sumner Williams.

The first half of this movie moves ahead like an express train barely able to stay on the tracks. It's absolutely relentless, teetering on the edge of the rails as it tears around each corner. Photographer George Diskant, one of the *noir* masters, along with Joseph Biroc and Burnett Guffey, lights and angles the scenes as if they were bop tenor solos, spurting and quaking and falling loose at the most unpredictable moments. And the music by Bernard Herrmann, who did so many Hitchcock scores, fractures the pictures, taking them apart and then rewelding them so that the pace hits home like a whirling, bucking bronc, each concussion shattering the previous mood or moment. When the plainclothes cops come filing into the room the camera perches at a point just below their belt buckles, so that as they enter and acknowledge their presence in the roll call it's as if they're trampling the cameraman/viewer like a herd of purposeful pachyderms.

Nicholas Ray, of course, is responsible for all of this. Crazy things, off-line, out-of-kilter things always happen in Ray's movies. He's far more predictable than Huston, say— somewhere in between Joseph Lewis and Robert Aldrich. Kind of like their half-crazy remittance man cousin. Here we have arch-cynical, overboiled city cop Robert Ryan, who's completely done in by his work. He can't stand the people he pushes up against, the hoods he's constantly forced to mangle and manhandle in order to squeeze information out of them like pus from a festering wound. He can no longer distinguish himself from the filth he handles. He won't socialize with "normal" people, won't court decent women, even though they go for him, because he's sick to death of everything: the world, in particular. It all looks like slime to him and he's dripping.

Ryan has one seminal scene that seizes the moment. He busts in on a grifter named Bernie who's holed up in a dockside hotel and just before Ryan beats the crap out of him, Ryan shudders and quakes, his voice breaks like Kirk Douglas's and he squeezes out, "Why do you punks make me do it? I'm gonna make you talk, you know you're gonna talk. So why do you make me do it?" There's so much self-hatred in this that it charges the film with a very personal, psychodramatic terror.

It's off the wall in a way that Ray's *Johnny Guitar* characters are, a sociopathic essay into darkness. And the weirdness of it can be humorous and deadly at the same time, as in the scene where Ryan quizzes Cleo Moore, a short, hot-stuff blonde, on the whereabouts of Bernie. Cleo sees that Ryan is fascinated by her assortment of perfumes and says, "Yeah, I like to stink myself up." She sprays herself with one. "This is called new-it de Paris. That means night of Paris," she tells him. Ryan has no sympathy for her or anyone else, and he twists her arm until she talks, knowing full well that Bernie or one of his pals will do worse when they find out she's squealed.

The second half of the movie is a different case altogether. Ryan is shipped off to the country by his boss Ed Begley to help out on a child murder. Begley thinks Ryan has gone off the deep end and could use a break. So Ryan gets involved with Ida Lupino, a blind woman who's protecting her demented younger brother, in a preposterous scenario, and the film loses much of its intensity. Ward Bond, as the crazed father of the murder victim, provides the foil off whom Ryan is able to bounce his own reflection. The ending is sappy and predictable; it was forced onto Ray by the studio, but he can't have been disappointed with the stunning first half. That forty-one minutes is as mesmerizing as any *noir* on film, unrelieved and difficult tension nobody will forget. Co-authored by the great A. I. Bezzerides (*Kiss Me Deadly* and *Thieves' Highway*).

On the Waterfront

1954. Directed by Elia Kazan. From an original screenplay by Budd Schulberg. Starring Marlon Brando, Eva Marie Saint, Rod Steiger, Lee J. Cobb, Karl Malden, and Leif Erickson.

The last time I was in Chicago, where I grew up, I ran into Jimmy Catolica, a former trainer and boxing promoter who once tended bar at Tony Zale's, a restaurant owned by the ex-middleweight champ located across the street from my father's store.

Jimmy's in his eighties now, a wizened little man with a thin wisp of white hair that rises from the top of his head like a toadstool. I asked him what had happened to Kid T-Bone, a welterweight he'd owned.

"Aw, he was gonna be a great one," Jimmy said. "Y'shoulda seen him against Aurelio right here at the Stockyards. Tore him right up. Aurelio couldn't read the big E for weeks after that one. He was on top until the Bighorn Johnson fight."

"What happened?" I asked.

Jimmy shrugged and tried to spit in the curb but he didn't have any spit. "He got married is what happened. That devil broad tore his guts out like Tiger Flowers couldn't have. Like Sandy Saddler couldn't have. Like Gavilan or Pep or Griffith in his prime when he wasn't makin' hats. Nobody. She took all his dough—the money I'd saved for him—and spread it up and down Michigan Avenue. When she was ready for the big time she pushed him into the match with Bighorn."

"Didn't you have control over that?" I asked.

Jimmy snickered and shook his wispy head. "With the poor guy pleading for more money all the time? I wanted him to go in with DiRoma, who he could have run and cut for twelve until they stopped it. DiRoma was an animal, he wouldn't have gone down, but T-Bone would have cut him to pieces. But we couldn't get the kind of money his saint of a life's companion needed from DiRoma. So we made the Johnson fight, which lasted all of five. Bighorn had the Bone down three times before that. She used everything she had so he wouldn't listen to me, Joey Falco, nobody."

"And after that?"

"What do you think? She left him. Took up with some sharp player in Camden or God knows. But T-Bone was finished. He didn't have any confidence left and he couldn't get it back. I got him in with a stiff named Dynamite Daley when Daley was a junkie and the Bone lasted six. Six! With a junkie! Got him Acie Akins and he went two. The last time was with Romulus Vincenzo in Jersey City and it was over before Falco could take the stool out of the ring. I don't even know where the Bone is now, if he's still alive. He went back to Mobile, I think, after Vincenzo put a permanent dent in his cheek, and I haven't seen or heard of him since. You never know with fighters."

Had Jimmy Catolica handled Terry Malloy, Malloy might have been somebody, maybe better than a contender; rather than a bum, which is, as Brando so poignantly played him, what he became. With guys like brother Charlie and Johnny Friendly in his corner, he didn't stand a chance even if he'd had the talent. To short-timers like them, the price on Wilson was impossible to pass up. *On the Waterfront* is about union corruption, sure, but it says more about the business of boxing without going near a ring than any boxing movie. Watch for Two Ton Tony Galento in a bit role as a union thug.

Out of the Past

1947. Directed by Jacques Tourneur. Based on the novel *Build My Gallows High* by Geoffrey Homes (Daniel Mainwaring, who also wrote the screenplay). Starring Robert Mitchum, Jane Greer, Kirk Douglas, Virginia Huston, Rhonda Fleming, Richard Webb, and Dickie Moore.

This is one of the most well-known *noir* melodramas, and deservedly so, because it's one of the best. The plot is overcomplicated but it works largely due to the smooth interplay of the cast and the deft manner in which director Tourneur runs them in and out like substitutions in a football game, always keeping a fresh back in to carry the ball.

Mitchum is making a new life for himself as Jeff Bailey, operating a filling station in a town in the Sierra foothills. He's courting a nice local girl and has a mute boy for an assistant. When a former crony passes through and recognizes him as Jeff Markham, private eye, the jig is up. The guy tells Mitchum the big boss, Kirk Douglas, for whom Mitchum once worked, wants to see him. Mitchum drives to Tahoe to see Douglas, and on the way relates his story to Ann, his girlfriend. Douglas had hired

Mitchum to track down his, Douglas's, mistress, Kathie (played by Jane Greer), who'd stolen $40,000 from him and skipped the country. Mitchum found her in Acapulco, but fell for her and they ran off together to San Francisco to live, Mitchum believing her story that she hadn't stolen the money. But of course she had, and following a bizarre series of events she winds up back with Douglas, leaving Mitchum in the cold. Greer is great as the conniving, sexy bitch, a terrific liar who tries to convince Mitchum that Douglas is keeping her with him in Tahoe now against her will. When Douglas tries to frame Mitchum for a couple of murders (one committed by Greer), he goes back to the little town in the mountains.

But Greer won't let him go. She persuades Mitchum to run off again with her but the cops come after them and they're killed. Mitchum has had his mute kid helper convey to Ann, Mitchum's nice girl, that he really loved Greer so that Ann can go on with her life, free of sad thoughts about him. This is all wildly improbable, as with most movies like it, but some of the scenes are absolutely brilliant and don't fade: most notably the Mexico sequence with Greer wrapping Mitchum around her finger, seducing him like some elegant reptile, repulsive but fascinating, swallowing him whole. Mitchum is a decent enough big lug, his sleepy expression disguising his excitement until Greer gives him the big bite and takes him down for the count. She's a spiky little vixen, sharp nails, eyes, edges. She sets up the picture so well, presenting herself as the sweetest piece of pussy in the western world, when it's obvious she's a super illusionist, doing more fucking with her mind than her body. A bad-news woman. No wonder Mitchum gets so disgusted, both with her and himself. He thinks he's not really good enough for the good Ann, and the only way he can square himself with himself is to throw her off him forever.

The classic shot here is of a bad dame dragging a good man down, but I don't buy it. Who says Mitchum is such a good scout in the first place? Forget the moralizing gesture and accept the scenery, the nasty turns of plot. Majestic mountains, tropical moonlight, foggy Frisco; Greer makes a great Cobra Woman and Mitchum the perfect foil. Remade as *Against All Odds* with Jeff Bridges and Rachel Ward, a movie devoid of soul, in which Jane Greer plays Rachel Ward's mother. Tourneur did it right the first time.

Pickup on South Street

1953. Directed by Samuel Fuller. Starring Jean Peters, Richard Widmark, Richard Kiley and Thelma Ritter.

This is arguably Sam Fuller's best picture, as well as Jean Peters's best role. I like it when lusciously beautiful women play down, act cheap and are good at it. This is one of the films that created the French *nouvelle vague* cinema. It's very European, really, in its long sequences, its music, its wan approach to life. Certainly a stark contrast to other American movies of the early '50s. The plot is a McCarthy Era potboiler: a cannon—a pickpocket—played by Widmark, lifts a wallet from a courier—Jean Peters—on a subway train in New York. The wallet contains a strip of microfilm that's headed into the hands of foreign agents. The Feds are trailing her and get derailed when the snatch is made. The rest of the play involves their finding him and recovering the microfilm. They make patriotic noise, separating grifting from the good of the country, etc., but the real business here is the ambience.

Sweaty, grainy black and white. Widmark, a three-time loser, lives in a bait shack on South Street under a bridge. A federal agent, aided by the New York City cops, locates Widmark (Skip McCoy) through a grass named Moe, played perfectly by Thelma Ritter. This is Ritter's best performance, even better than her turn as Bette Davis's assistant in *All About Eve*. Moe is a snitch, but a respected one. As Widmark says, "Moe's gotta eat, too." She's saving up to buy a classy burial plot on Long Island. "It would just about kill me," she says, to be buried in Potter's

Field. Ironically, it's Widmark, whom she's fingered, who saves Moe from just that fate.

The best and most beautiful scene in the movie is where Moe comes back late at night to her Bowery room—she sells bad ties for a dollar each—snaps on a light, kicks off her shoes from her tired feet, turns on the phonograph to play a sentimental old fake-French tune, flops down on the bed, and only then notices a man's shoed feet propped next to her. It's all done in one continuous shot, with the camera moving to accommodate her own movements, giving her enough room, and ending in a grand sigh. Moe is confronted by Richard Kiley, the traitor who sent Peters on the mission in the first place, and of course it ends with his murdering her. "I'm so tired, mister," Moe says. "You'd be doing me a big favor by just shooting me in the head." But she won't tell Kiley what's going on, how the cops have Peters and where Widmark lives. Moe's a patriot. The phony Frenchman's voice comes up, the deadly sentimentality of the scene overwhelms even the ghosts of Edith Piaf and Maurice Chevalier, and Moe catches a fast freight on the railway to grifters' heaven.

Jean Peters, who later married Howard Hughes, looks great here. She's a pushover, an easy dame, who's doing a last favor for ex-boyfriend Kiley. She falls for snakey Skip McCoy, even though he treats her worse than Kiley does, but that's what turns her on. And she acts the part without a hitch. The only minor flaw here is that she pronounces Houston Street like the city; in New York, they say "How-stun" Street. I don't understand how Fuller, an East Coast guy, could have let that one slip by. It's like Bogart in *Key Largo,* saying Key West con*ch* instead of "conk." Happens to the best of 'em, I guess.

Raging Bull (See *City for Conquest*)

Rebel Without a Cause

1955. Directed by Nicholas Ray. Starring James Dean, Natalie Wood, Sal Mineo, Jim Backus, Corey Allen, Dennis Hopper, Ann Doran, Nick Adams, and William Hopper.

Credit Nick Ray with this one all the way. Hollywood takes Robert Lindner's psychological study of American teenagers and decides to make it into a juvenile delinquent exploitation film. Like Woody Allen rerouting the book *Everything You Always Wanted to Know About Sex*. What we get from Ray is Greek tragedy. And the further tragic real-life connection is that all of the main players in the movie died young, as well as some of the supporting characters: Dean, Wood, Mineo, Nick Adams, are gone—the latter two in rather unsavory ways. Corey Allen, who plays Buzz Gunderson, the gang leader killed early in the movie during the chicken-run, directs religious television shows. Even William Hopper died relatively young.

Rebel focuses on well-to-do middle- to upper-middle-class kids; these aren't the Blackstone Rangers or Devil's Disciples here. The good weather in L.A. is tough on the guys—I mean, they have to wear those heavy leather jackets despite the fact it's so hot out. I really like the touch of having Sal Mineo, the young rich boy ignored by his parents, ride a motor scooter, a Vespa. The others all have cars, not motorcycles. They're just out for kicks. Their parents' safe lives bore them. The theme of *Rebel* is boredom. Anything for a yuck. Nick Ray suffuses the whole scene in a red glow, from the horizon right down to Dean's famous red windbreaker. Everybody's *so* sensitive here. But we don't really get to the bottom of this. What's concentrated on is the budding love affair between Dean and Wood, the fetal-shaped genuflection (i.e., submissive sex slave) by Mineo toward Dean, the stupid cops who just *have* to shoot somebody. It looks like nobody works for a living or will ever need to. Jim Backus has a great scene where he cleans up a spilled food tray wearing an apron, jabbering like Mr. Magoo. This really gets to his son, Jim (Dean), who implores him to stand up like a man, not only at the moment but also to his nagging wife (Doran) and mother-in-law. Jim doesn't seem to pay much attention to homework, doesn't have a job, but he has a car, nice clothes, etc.

These kids are the forerunners of the 1980s suburban kids who have to be driven everywhere, get bored easily unless they have a video game in their laps, and usually have at least two homes—divorce becoming so well-accepted that by now more than 50% of all American marriages break up within three to seven years. As a result, the chilren of these multivarious unions have got to be confused and angry and seek respite in electronic diversions. They're usually good at math, too. I mean, one and one equals two (most of the time); nothing to argue about, nothing to interpret. Mom's version and dad's version notwithstanding, either the starship got blasted or it didn't. No need to take sides, to be made to feel like a tennis ball. And everybody wants to be so skinny! The '80s have a stronger link to the '50s than fashions: there's even more crap to absorb and rebel against, and if possible it's even easier to feel unloved, un-wanted, and useless. All of which adds up to *la vie noire*.

Repulsion

1965. Directed by Roman Polanski. Starring Catherine Deneuve, Ian Hendry, Patrick Wymark, and Yvonne Furneaux.

Cul-de-Sac

1966. Directed by Roman Polanski. Starring Françoise Dorleac, Donald Pleasance, Lionel Stander, and Jacqueline Bisset.

Modern *noir*-horror at its best. Polanski's entire life seems to have been nothing but one strange interlude after another, so it's no mystery as to the genesis of his macabre pair, *Repulsion* and *Cul-de-Sac*. Not only are they sister films, but each stars one of a pair of real life sisters, Deneuve and Dorleac. Shortly after filming *Cul-de-Sac*, Françoise Dorleac, the older sister, was decapitated à la Jayne Mansfield in a car wreck; and then Polan-ski's wife, Sharon Tate, was murdered by the Manson family. What was it Charlie Manson used to say? What goes around, comes around.

Repulsion, filmed in London, is a bloody study of one young woman's madness. Deneuve is the younger sister of Yvonne

Furneaux, with whom she lives. When Furneaux and her boy-friend make love Deneuve lies stiff in her bed, listening to the sounds through the wall. It's all beyond her; she's terrified. Furneaux goes off for a weekend and all hell breaks loose. Deneuve cracks up totally and kills everything that walks into the apartment. The best murder is when she slits the landlord's throat. Patrick Wymark can't believe that this beautiful, nubile bird he's just made a pass at has cut him ear to ear, and he rushes to look in the mirror before his head topples off and she completes a job Norman Bates would have been proud of. Hands come through the walls, everything gets gooey, sexual, raw. By the time Furneaux and her amour return on Sunday night, the place is an absolute shambles. Dead men lie everywhere, even in the bathtub; blood is streaked on the walls and along the floor. Deneuve is in a catatonic state under the couch. The camera eye zooms in on her mad, distracted eyes in a family photo.

Polanski's use of black and white is so effective that the blood seems to be red, vivid red. He sets up each scene perfectly, introducing just enough humor or matter-of-fact behavior to get the viewer off guard. It's the same in *Cul-de-Sac*, which is black comedy with bullets. Two wounded gangsters take refuge in a castle in the French countryside owned by Donald Pleasance and his sexy young wife, Dorleac. It's a beautiful moment when she awakes one morning, pulls on tight blue jeans and a sweater over her slender body, and walks out of the room. Nothing could be more perfect than the way she looks and moves, and then the shit hits the fan and everybody goes belly up. Stander is fantastic, trying to fool dinner guests by acting as a servant with a busted arm, talking in his gravelly voice. It's a grand send-up, an unfairly-ignored piece of comic *noir* that owes a true debt to Lubitsch, the first great Polish filmmaker, but makes some points purely for Polanski as well. Polanski's later efforts in this vein, such as *The Tenant* (awful), and *The Fearless Vampire Killers* (some good moments but chaotic), don't cohere. *Cul-de-Sac* could remain his masterwork in this genre. And *Repulsion* is just simply more horrifying than anything Hitchcock ever made. Truffaut fell terribly short in this field (*The Bride Wore Black* and *Confidentially Yours*); he was better by far with autobiographical material, although *The Soft Skin*, which also starred Françoise Dorleac, is a deft, brutally honest attempt. Maybe that's why Polanski's so good at it.

Road House

1948. Directed by Jean Negulesco. Starring Richard Widmark, Cornel Wilde, Ida Lupino, Celeste Holm, and O. Z. Whitehead.

What I like about this movie is the pretense itself, the ultraphony *noir* attitude, the hokey sets (especially for the outdoor scenes), and Ida Lupino's unparalleled drop-dead persona that comes off as screenwriter/producer Edward Chodorov's *idea* of hardboiled patter. Nothing really flows in this; it struts, parades, excites, tantailizes, oozes, and dies in absurd melodramatics. However, Ida Lupino is remarkable as the torch singer/pianist who's brought to the sticks from the Big Town by roadhouse owner Widmark at a big salary because he digs her and wants to marry her. He can't get into her pants, though, and that forces him to push harder. Of course she falls in love with Cornel Wilde, Widmark's partner in the bar-lounge/bowling alley, a rustic-moderne barn of a place out on the lost highway somewhere in the upper Midwest.

There is a strange quality about the film, like a plastic coating underneath which the characters struggle. The story is a setup, the eternal triangle plus the good dame, played to the nth degree by veteran second fiddle Celeste Holm; but the seethrough/undersea illusion is courtesy of photographer Joseph La Shelle, whose black and white expressiveness defies colorization. Wilde's character is established early on as fussy; he's the nuts and bolts guy in the partnership. He tries to get rid of Lupino right away but she balks and stands her ground. She annoys Wilde by allowing her cigarettes to burn down on the piano; he's always wiping up after her or trying to get her to use an ashtray.

At the same time he's obviously the big beef heartthrob of the movie, a curious contrast of types. Clifton Webb could have done this role to death, and it would have been a real hoot to see Ida go for *him*! Meanwhile, Widmark is off in the ozone while Wilde/Lupino consummate their relationship. Lupino, who does her own singing, is campy wonderful, with her raspy lark talk bringing in the crowds. There's a howl of a scene when Wilde tries to teach Lupino how to bowl and she keeps throwing gutter balls on purpose. Wilde is like a prissy Victor Mature, if you can imagine that. It's this off-center part of his character that's most interesting.

And of course Widmark ends up crazed, doing his Tommy Udo mad act straight out of *Kiss of Death*. When he discovers Wilde and Lupino are a duo, Widmark sets Wilde up for a fall, framing him for a nonexistent theft. Wilde goes to trial, but as the judge is about to sentence him to state prison, Widmark intervenes and convinces the judge to parole Wilde in his custody. That way he can keep Lupino and Wilde prisoner, torturing them with his manipulative behavior and shrieking laughter. Finally, he contrives a scheme whereby he can set the couple up for a lam across the border, so that he can hunt them down and kill Wilde. (Earler in the movie Widmark brags to Celeste Holm that he bagged three moose on a hunting trip.) This scenario plays itself out but the tables get turned and it's the wigged-out Widmark who takes the pipe, thanks especially to the women, who are the real heroes of this top-heavy tragedy. Ida Lupino came a long way in a real hurry from *Little Women*. In fact, they could have called this one *Jo's Boys in Hell*.

Scarlet Street

1945. Directed by Fritz Lang. Based on Jean Renoir's film, *La Chienne*, which was an adaptation of the play and novel of the same title by Georges de la Fouchardière and Mouezy-Eon. Starring Edward G. Robinson, Joan Bennett, Dan Duryea, and Margaret Lindsay.

Lang and Robinson do a pretty good job to come up to the standard set by Renoir and Michel Simon. Robinson plays a mousey clerk who's worked his entire life for one company. On the night of his testimonial dinner, at which he's presented with a gold watch, he sees a man beating a woman on a street corner as he's walking home. Chris (Robinson) runs to help the woman and the man takes off. The girl is sexy Joan Bennett, named Kitty, and Chris walks her to her door. It's obvious to Kitty that Chris is a mark, and she encourages him to come back and see her. Chris is married to a harridan named Millie who is constantly extolling the virtues of her first husband, whom she thinks is dead. She pesters and carps continually at Chris, bugging him about his messy Sunday painting, telling him over and over how worthless both he and the paintings are.

So Chris begins courting Kitty, who is encouraged to hustle him by her no-good boyfriend, Johnny, played by Dan Duryea, the same guy who was swatting her when Chris came along. Both Johnny and Kitty are indolent, amoral characters, and Kitty prick-teases Chris for everything she and Johnny want. She introduces Johnny to Chris as her cousin or brother when he first catches them together. Chris is blinded by his passion for Kitty, and embezzles funds from his company to satisfy her, setting her up in a fancy Greenwich Village apartment, which he decorates with his own paintings. It's also a place for him to work, and he begins a large portrait of his new muse, Kitty. Johnny starts peddling the paintings, however, passing them off as Kitty's. She becomes a big celebrity and the paintings sell well. Chris discovers what's happening but Kitty coos in his ear and calms him, saying it's all a misunderstanding and she'll straighten it out. He's so mad for her that he relents. Then his horrible wife's first husband turns up and Chris realizes he's free to marry Kitty and rushes to her. Of course she's making love with Johnny and Chris goes berserk, stabbing her to death with an icepick. Johnny gets away but the cops catch up with him and convict him for Kitty's murder. Meanwhile, Chris's firm discovers his embezzlement and rather than press charges they take into consideration his long service and merely dismiss him. He's out on the street and can't attempt to sell his paintings because the world thinks they're the work of the murdered Kitty. Chris is a broken man, doomed to become a bum.

I like almost all of Lang's movie: the slick New York streets, flashing black and white night shadows and contrasts; the contemptible behavior of Kitty and Johnny, and the meek, masochistic Chris. But the ending pales compared to Renoir's treatment: there we see Simon years later, a bum but one at peace with himself, watching rich people carry off a painting for which they've paid an enormous sum, one of his. Simon manages to laugh at it all—the folly of his life, the folly of everyone's life. It's no less mean an existence, he's saying, but less bleak and self-pitying than Lang's disposition of Chris. "La chienne" translates as "the bitch," who emerges here as a triumvirate: wife, mistress, and life itself.

Série Noire

1981. Directed by Alain Corneau. Based on the novel *A Hell of a Woman* by Jim Thompson. Starring Patrick Dewaere.

This is definitely the best movie made from a Jim Thompson novel to date. Bertrand Tavernier's version of Thompson's *Pop. 1280, Coup de Torchon (Clean Slate)*, was wonderful, largely due to the performance of Philippe Noiret, but Patrick Dewaere, as a demented thief/murderer/child molester, is as close to a real Jim Thompson character as an actor could get. His frenzied behavior, deranged notion of right and wrong, suit Thompson's sense of satire, his nightmarish vision of Man's Fate.

I first saw Dewaere in *Les Valseuses (Going Places)*, a Bertrand Blier movie costarring Gerard Depardieu and Jeanne Moreau. Dewaere and Depardieu play a couple of oafs on the road, dunderhead Dean Moriarty and Sal Paradise; Dewaere stole the show there, making the viewer sympathetic to him despite his horrid behavior. Dewaere's was a vulnerable, palpitating screen presence, and it's a shame he's gone: Dewaere committed suicide not long after the filming of *Série Noire*. In it, he plays a salesman who calls on a house occupied by an old woman and her granddaughter. The old woman makes a practice of offering the young girl sexually to bill collectors, salesmen, and so on, in exchange for goods, the light bill, whatever's necessary. Dewaere goes for it, too, but finds out from the girl that the old crone has a fortune hidden in her mattress. He conspires with the girl, Mona, to murder the woman and steal the money. Dewaere is married but doesn't get along with his wife; theirs is a comic-tragic relationship, the kind where neither of them really ever speaks directly to the other. And Dewaere never tells her what's going on in his life.

Dewaere recruits a big dumb friend of his to do the killing, and in the horrible process of clubbing and shooting the big guy is killed, too. Now Dewaere has the money but he also has the girl, to whom he has become sexually addicted. But she drives him nuts because she doesn't really speak. She's not fully developed, her mind is a cipher, and this drives Dewaere crazier than he already is. Now all this is quite different from the Thompson novel on which the movie is based, a book that ends in suicide and/or castration and involves many more people than Corneau presents. However, Corneau has captured the essence of Thompson's depraved beings. Dewaere is saddled with a moron; he can't abide his own bad judgment, his own greed. Nothing works out, Thompson tells us, and it never has to, never. Not only will other people let you down, but you'll disappoint yourself, too. It's a bleak vision, true, but no other writer examined the downside so thoroughly, so relentlessly. Dewaere's agitation, his twisted expressions, illustrate perfectly the frustration inherent in Thompson's world-view. It's unsettling, to say the least—fascinating albeit horrifying to witness. Sex, money, murder, greed—a lovely bunch of coconuts. *Série Noire* is like a malevolent *King of Hearts*, with the lunatics taking asylum amongst the population. Nobody's safe, says Jim Thompson, and Corneau, with the aid of Dewaere, managed to show us why.

The Set-Up (See *City for Conquest*)

Shack Out on 101

1955. Directed by Edward Dein. Starring Terry Moore, Lee Marvin, Keenan Wynn, and Frank Lovejoy.

The secret of this movie is that nobody has to act in it. And it's a good thing, too, because neither Terry Moore nor Frank Lovejoy could if they had to. Lee Marvin and Keenan Wynn, however, give their usual hammy, amusing performances, and the whole thing is low-key enough that nobody gets stepped on. What comes out of this silly little Red Scare spy drama from the smack-dab middle of the 1950s is an almost perfect, semi-trashy set piece; everybody has a good time.

The setting is a beanery near a missile base owned by Wynn. Marvin is the short-order cook, Moore is the Tomato, and Lovejoy, as usual, is the humorless Fed out to uncover the spy. As Lovejoy goes through his "Meet McGraw" routine, Wynn works out with weights, Moore displays her lovely breasts in a sweater, and Marvin grunts and leers and makes unwholesome suggestions to her. It's as if William Inge were forced by the government to rewrite some Chekhov play, but set in McCarthy-era America, and he took twenty Valium, washed them down with Old Crow, and dashed it off as the drug grabbed his brain and put him in Palookaville.

It doesn't matter who the spy really is; everyone sits around on stools and makes comments not unlike the characters in the Arizona café in *The Petrified Forest*. People going through life half-awake, half-aware, unfinished, unsure of how to handle destiny's nagging reminders. They poke at one another, spook away, there's an occasional shove. The government guy is always the stupid one, the real pawn, the one who follows orders. All The Tomato wants is some flash jerk to drag her off down Highway 101 to L.A. where she can shop and go to the beach. Wynn is a guy who knows his limitations. Lovejoy's a blank. Marvin's the only interesting one here. This movie is a dead-on minimalist portrait of America at its most paranoid. It's the one to show the history class.

Shadow of a Doubt

1943. Directed by Alfred Hitchcock. Starring Teresa Wright, Joseph Cotten, Macdonald Carey, Henry Travers, Wallace Ford, Hume Cronyn, and Patricia Collinge.

Hitchcock liked to make movies in Northern California, especially in small communities such as Bodega Bay (*The Birds*) and Santa Rosa, where *Shadow of a Doubt* was filmed. In 1943, Santa Rosa was a model small American town, right out of Frank Capra. It may as well have been in New England or Iowa or Pennsylvania for all the relation it bears to California in this movie. One would never know there was a war going on at the time, either; that 100,000 Japanese-Americans had just been carted off from Santa Rosa and other California cities to concentration camps in remote areas of the West. Everything seems so calm, sedate, harmless. Big families live in picturebook gabled high-windowed houses on serene, well-kept streets. Like kids' grammar school readers. Not a thing to get upset about, nothing out of place. The lie seems complete.

Enter Evil. This time it's in the form of Uncle Charlie, played by Joseph Cotten, the prodigal relative come to Santa Rosa to visit for a while, maybe to settle down. The world traveler, who also happens to be the "Merry Widow Murderer," a guy who robs and kills matronly ladies. We see him elude the cops in a tawdry section of an eastern city, something like Baltimore. He takes the train out west to see his sister and her family, which includes his favorite niece—Teresa Wright—who's also named

Charlie, after him. Dad, played by cutesy old loveable Henry Travers (Clarence the Angel in Capra's *It's a Wonderful Life*), wife, and kids all greet Uncle Charlie effusively—their rich, mysterious relation. Charlie makes himself comfortable, not really knowing the cops are hot on his trail. He's cautious, suspicious, but figures he's outwitted the authorities; after all, he's a genius of sorts, too good for most people. Charlie's an oddball but his niece worships him, and his sister can't do enough for him.

Little by little niece Charlie is alienated by her uncle; he has mean moments that nobody else seems to notice. She discovers he's cut an article on the Merry Widow Murderer out of the paper. He fits the description. Undercover cops come to town, and one—Macdonald Carey—falls for young Charlie. He manages to enlist her in capturing Cotten. At first she resists, but then her kind uncle locks her in a garage with an automobile engine running and she nearly suffocates. The peaceful little town becomes a nightmarish setting. Neighbor Hume Cronyn, a buddy of her dad's, is a pulp mystery freak; his speculation on the motivation of murderers and quest for the perfect crime irritate Uncle Charlie, and he begins to come apart. He has to escape, but he knows his niece is on to him, so he tries to throw her off his departing train. In one of the classic sequences in movie history, it's Uncle Charlie who falls prey to a passing speeding locomotive.

Hitchcock's mastery of contrasts is never more evident than in this movie; into each life a little rain must fall, and afterwards everything seems fine again, but it never is. At least not for anyone who has something to lose.

Shock Corridor

1963. Directed by Samuel Fuller. Starring Peter Breck, Constance Towers, Gene Evans, James Best, Hari Rhodes, Philip Ahn, and Larry Tucker.

Shock Corridor was playing at a classic cinema theater in Paris in 1967 when I first saw the title, prominently displayed on the marquee. I couldn't resist it and bought a ticket for the next show. I had seen Samuel Fuller's *House of Bamboo, Pickup on South Street,* and *The Crimson Kimono* as a kid, but I didn't recognize his name as the director. *Corridor* turned out to be completely different than the others, far more bizarre and sleazy. Fuller created a fascinatingly lurid, cheap paperback of a movie. In fact, it bears more than a passing similarity to Jim Thompson's early '50s novel, *The Alcoholics.*

Johnny Barratt, played by Peter Breck, is an investigative journalist obsessed with winning a Pulitzer Prize. He convinces his newspaper editor to let him get himself admitted to a local mental hospital as a patient in order to solve a murder. It's the Nellie Bly trick, and Johnny figures this will make him famous. His girlfriend, Cathy (Constance Towers), is a stripper, and Johnny persuades her to lie on his behalf to get him admitted, to tell the head doctor that she's Johnny's sister and that he keeps making sexual advances to her. Johnny is coached by a doctor friend of his editor in order to give "correct" answers to the mental-hospital doctor, and finally Johnny is taken in as a patient.

Once inside the nuthouse, of course, everything changes. Johnny really begins to go crazy. Three of the inmates witnessed the murder and Johnny attempts to quiz them individually. He makes some progress, finding out it was one of the attendants who killed the guy, but Johnny becomes convinced Cathy is making it with other guys while he's trapped in the bin. He has strange dreams, nightmares in which he's at the far end of a long tunnel, visions of Cathy coming on to other men. He's over-whelmed by paranoid delusions and soon is as victimized by his surroundings as the others. He's awakened during the middle of the night by an obese patient nicknamed Pagliacci, who sits on Johnny's chest and sings arias, conducts operas only he can hear, and stuffs wads of gum into Johnny's mouth. This kind of behav-ior is common in prisons and asylums, only it's usually a cock being shoved into the sleeping victim, not gum.

Two of the murder witnesses are too far gone to help Johnny

uncover the killer, one of whom is a black man who's convinced he's a white Ku Klux Klan member (he'd been a James Meredith-type lone black student at an all-white college); another thinks he's a Confederate soldier (he'd been a traitor during the Korean War). The third, Boden (Gene Evans), is a scientist who helped develop the atomic bomb and then looned out, leaving him with the mind of a child. Boden does come across, however, and tells Johnny the name of the murderer.

By this time Johnny's completely bonkers. He's been attacked not only by Pagliacci, but by a gang of nymphomaniacs from the women's compound, and given shock treatments (at Cathy's suggestion!) when he comes to believe he really is Cathy's brother. He even loses his voice. Finally, he's able to expose the asylum guard as the killer, for which Johnny will probably win the Pulitzer Prize, but he's hopelessly insane now and the achievement means nothing to him.

The whole movie is crazy, and cheap besides. Fuller's attempts at exposing the social and moral failings of American society are gross, heavyhanded, and predictable. But the movie is zany and farfetched enough to overcome its faults. Cathy the striptease queen comes off as the sanest person in the group, as well as strangely sexless. The mental hospital, like Jim Thompson's fictional sanitarium El Healtho, is cartoonish, but the brutality of the place is rendered as vividly as it was in Val Lewton's *Bedlam* (1946), and is just as frightening. The French, of course, take these satires as evidence—literal exposés of American life—and they're no more than half wrong, maybe less.

Shoot the Piano Player

1962. Directed by François Truffaut. Based on the novel *Down There* by David Goodis. Starring Charles Aznavour, Marie Dubois, Michele Mercier, and Nicole Berger.

David Goodis was, according to literary critic Geoffrey O'Brien, "the poet of the lost." Goodis specialized in stories involving men and women on their uppers, the down-and-out, and down-for-the-count types struggling to find some small way in which to justify their existence; a hint, a suggestion, a clue as to why or how to go on living. In most cases, they're unable to find a satisfactory answer and the bottom comes up fast to greet them. Extremely popular as a novelist in France, the subject of a popular biography, and perpetually in print as a staple of Gallimard's *Série Noire*, Goodis's books have been largely unavailable in his native country since the 1950s. Born in Philadelphia, where he also died, David Goodis lived mostly with his mother except for a brief period when he worked on screenplays in Hollywood. Decent films of his works were turned out there: *Nightfall* and *Dark Passage* are two of the better ones. But the best job was done by Truffaut with *Down There*, retitled *Shoot the Piano Player (Tirez sur la Pianiste)*.

Charles Aznavour portrays Charlie Koller, formerly Edouard Saroyan, a honkytonk piano player, slapping out dance tunes for sloshed patrons in a workingmans bar; as Saroyan (the name chosen by Aznavour after another famous Armenian), he was a great concert pianist who played the finest halls around the world. Part of the story, of course, is how and why he came to sink so low, but the action involves the circumstances of the life he's come to live. Charlie lives with his ten-year-old son in a crummy apartment in a poor section of town. He has a simpatico relationship with his neighbor, a prostitute who likes Charlie and gives it to him for free. Charlie drifts along until he falls in love with a barmaid at the joint he's working in; and they soon become involved in the world of his brothers, a gang of thieves operating out of the family farmhouse. One of the brothers shows up at the bar one night and asks Charlie to help him hide out, to get away from some bad guys who are after him. Charlie doesn't want to get into it, but he can't refuse. He assists his brother and now the thugs come after him. They kidnap his boy and terrorize Marie Dubois, Charlie's lovely new girlfriend. He's reluctantly involved in the real world again, and again things go wrong.

With the use of flashbacks, Truffaut shows us how Charlie came to reject his former life: his pretty wife, played by Michele Mercier, got him his shot at stardom by clandestinely sleeping with the top concert promoter. She keeps this a secret from Edouard/Charlie, but their relationship goes sour; the secret gnaws at her, they draw apart, and finally she commits suicide. This is enough to put him on the rocks. He's warmed anew by sweet Marie, but the gangsters put an end to that, too, and everything unravels again. One of the most touching and beautiful scenes in movie history is when Marie is shot and rolls over and over down a snowy hill.

There's no use, says Goodis, no way to avoid the shit, *la merde*, and Truffaut remains true to Goodis's point of view. The way he does it, though, is so poetic, so tender, that it seems to make sense, like going under on some luxurious drug. That roll down the hill is utterly sensual; the beautiful girl dead in Charlie's arms with snow in her hair. The thugs are buffoons, yes, stupid, stepping on the innocent flower. Nobody gets left alone, ever.

Some Came Running

1958. Directed by Vincente Minnelli. Starring Frank Sinatra, Shirley MacLaine, Dean Martin, Martha Hyer and Arthur Kennedy.

Deadline at Dawn

1946. Directed by Harold Clurman. Screenplay by Clifford Odets from the novel by Cornell Woolrich. Starring Bill Williams, Susan Hayward, Paul Lukas, Joseph Calleia, Marvin Miller, Lola Lane, Osa Masson and Jerome Cowan.

Some Came Running is one of the wonderful bad movies of all time. It's absolutely, 100% American in concept and execution, a perfectly awful evocation of post-World War II small town USA. It does James Jones's novel, on which the film is based, sufficient justice, taking the verbose 1,100 + pages of the book and wringing from it a strawberry red tattoo of a picture. Sinatra, still wearing the same uniform he wore as Maggio in *From Here To Eternity* (1953), tries to go home again and finds out he never had one, which he'd suspected all along. He hooks up with small-time gambler Dean Martin, the terror of cheap women and backroom card parlors from Springfield to Visalia. (There's a Springfield and/or a Visalia in every state throughout the midwest.) But it's MacLaine who steals the show, as a dumb bunny broad from Chicago who tags after Sinatra (she even has a pink bunny purse). Martin, as 'Bama Dillert, or whatever the hell his name is, calls her a pig, and Frank stands up for her, even though he's been trying to get rid of her. This establishes him as a decent-enough guy, in contrast to his slimy grocery-clerk mentality brother, played by Arthur Kennedy, whose wife is a greedy bitch, and who is having an affair with his secretary.

Kennedy's daughter idolizes Frank, because he once wrote a novel, though he says he's quit the writing game. Frank also makes out with Martha Hyer, a classy local dame who teaches at the college and who tries to get him to go back to the typewriter and stop drinking so much. Frank, as Dave Hirsh, has low self-esteem, as the psychologists say, but he's a moral sonofabitch to the end, unlike 'Bama, who is a stand-up guy but intolerant as hell. 'Bama never takes off his half-Stetson hat, even in bed, which is a good touch. The color in the film gets redder and redder as it goes along, just as the story line and dialogue get progressively more purple. The tail begins wagging the dog after about an hour and a half (running time of the movie is 127 minutes, and you can feel every one of them like back spasms after the first ninety), just like the book. But this is real Americana, circa the late '40s to mid-'50s, genuine narrow-mindedness served up soup kitchen-style.

For some strange reason, every time I see *Deadline At Dawn* I'm reminded of *Some Came Running*. Maybe because it involves a sailor on a 24-hour leave who gets mixed up in a situation he could have avoided if he'd stayed at sea, the way Dave Hirsh could have avoided Peyton Place had he re-upped in the army. *Deadline* has a speechifying script by Odets that doesn't fit the Woolrich story but there's enough spooky big-city weirdness left in to satisfy. The best bit is the customer in the dime-a-dance hall who wears gloves while he dances with Susan Hayward. He creeps her out and she gets him eighty-sixed after he admits he has a disease. Bill Williams is the innocent, the naive sailor who falls into a pit of disease, from alcoholic tramp women to murder. It's the Big Town, New York, not small town Illinois here, as in *Some Came Running*, but it's the same vicious mess and no way to avoid stepping in the sludge.

Marvin Miller has a wonderful part in *Deadline* as Sleepy Parsons, the blind ex-husband of the miserable wench who preys on young men. Miller was an underrated actor who usually played a heavy in movies in the 1940s, such as *Dead Reckoning* (1947). He made a name for himself as the spokesman and representative for the fictional philanthropist John Beresford Tipton in the '50s television series, *The Millionaire.*

Despair is the central theme of both movies. No way out of either place, large or small. Soldier and sailor are better off in the service, in the barracks or on board ship. The cities and towns are infested with rats that bite, and bite some more. They crawl up your pantslegs and shit on your shoes. Shoot one and another springs up. These movies make America look like purgatory from which only the noblest will escape. Charles Williams would have titled these stories *Sin Town* and *Sin City,* a pair of four-bit Gold Medal yarns off the wire rack in the Trailways coffee shop.

Somebody Up There Likes Me

(See *City for Conquest*)

Straight Time

1978. Directed by Ulu Grosbard. Based on the novel *No Beast So Fierce* by Edward Bunker. Starring Dustin Hoffman, Harry Dean Stanton, Emmett Walsh, Theresa Russell, and Gary Busey.

An almost-on-the-money movie, betrayed by poor editing and a few plot flaws, *Straight Time* nonetheless is fascinating and truthful in a way seldom evoked in movies or anywhere else in the arts. Hoffman is a semi-sleazy, weasely little guy released after six years in prison. He's a lifetime criminal, a petty thief who ends up a killer, but a guy who does not have a clue as to how one survives in the straight world. Straight life holds no excitement, no thrills. On the street he teams up with old pals who are equally bored by jobs: Harry Dean Stanton can't stand being a small success as a businessman with a backyard pool in the suburbs; Gary Busey has to mainline heroin to keep from blowing his top while he struggles to work a nine-to-five to support his wife and kid. These guys need action, and sometimes anything will do.

In Hoffman's case, as Max Dembo, he needs to get caught, too, and that complicates things for his buddies, who end up dead because of it. Dembo hooks up with a pretty young girl who has nothing much going on in her life and allows herself to be part of his destructive pattern of behavior. Dembo is victimized by his jerkoff parole officer, played with perfect sleazoid skill by Emmett Walsh, and that sets Dembo off; but he's really hopeless, incorrigible, a guy who won't ever fit in and he is more aware of that than anyone. Dembo is so desperate to get off that he's ready to try to take a poker game in a motel without the proper firepower. Stanton saves him by insisting it's "unprofessional" to go in without a shotgun. So Dembo drives to a gun store, breaks in at four A.M., and steals a shotgun. He's nuts, but gentle with the girl; in fact, he has no desire to *harm* anyone. When Busey chickens out as the driver in a jewelry robbery, Dembo does what he thinks is the right thing, especially as Stanton gets killed because of it; he offs Busey. Dembo's only doing what's honorable, *deserved*.

This is a troubling movie; it doesn't make it all the way and yet it nags, gnaws on the viewer like food that just won't digest. It's difficult to watch someone you can't really completely dislike—a character as non-heroic as Dembo—and watch him mess up on purpose and take everyone around him down too. The only place for him is jail; he's too far along now, an inbetween soul. Hoffman does a serious and fine job with this, but the history of this movie is that it was never properly completed, and was edited without the approval of Hoffman so he disowned the product as released. But Harry Dean Stanton is terrific, as usual; especially in the scene where he and Hoffman are sitting around eating hamburgers in Stanton's suburban backyard and as soon as his wife is out of earshot he begs Hoffman to get him out of there. Gary Busey is perfect, too, as the weak link junkie, big and goofy and pathetic. Theresa Russell is lovely and vulnerable, perfectly frightened and drifting. They're all okay, and even if it doesn't quite add up *Straight Time* is a powerful and disturbing little film, certainly *noir* enough for anyone.

The Strange Love of Martha Ivers

1946. Directed by Lewis Milestone. Starring Van Heflin, Barbara Stanwyck, Kirk Douglas, Lizabeth Scott, Darryl Hickman, and Judith Anderson.

This movie is filled with darkness, brown soot, pessimism, secrecy, control freaks. Barely adolescent Martha Ivers plans to run away from Iverstown and her nasty rich aunt, played by Judith Anderson. Martha and her buddy Sam Masterson are discovered in a boxcar before they can get away and Martha's taken home. Back at the gloomy mansion, Martha confronts her aunt on a staircase during a power failure in a thunderstorm, cracks her on the head with a cane, and kills her. With Martha is the son of her live-in tutor, Walter, who supports Martha's story that an intruder murdered her aunt and then ran out the front door, which the tutor finds wide open. Young Sam Masterson had snuck into the house but was hiding under the stairs when Martha clocked the old lady, so didn't see what happened. He takes off before the cops arrive.

Eighteen years later, Sam Masterson returns to Iverstown. As Sam, Van Heflin is world-weary but clever enough to know how to stay out of trouble he can't handle. Iverstown was always bad news for him, and he paints it as an unfriendly place to a sailor he's given a lift to. It amuses Sam to be back, however; he's a cynic, anyway, and hasn't found the rest of the world to be a much more pleasant ride than his old hometown. He picks up right away on a cute blonde, Toni Marachek, played by Lizabeth Scott. Toni's destitute, just out of jail in fact, and the local authorities want her out of town. Sam takes her in as if she were a bird with a wounded wing—not in an aggressive, sexual way. He bumps into his old girlfriend Martha (Stanwyck) who's now married to Walter (Kirk Douglas). Walter's the D.A. and Martha inherited her aunt's fortune, so she runs the town and uses her husband as a tool. She and Walter think Sam might know the real story of the murder, so Walter tries to use Toni as a pawn to get Sam in trouble and out of the way. Sam, meanwhile, trades on his earlier friendship with Martha to find out the true story about the murder. When Sam starts playing up to Martha, Walter gets hot and wants to destroy Masterson; but Walter's an impotent alcoholic, and Sam's street savvy saves him. He and Toni beat it and Martha and Walter wind up a double suicide.

Nice story, yes? Nobody is happy in this, not even a little bit. Rich or poor it's all the same take. Car mechanics, gamblers, cops, lawyers, old people walking their dogs in the park, all ugly, sad, and mean. It's a very dark vision of the world, set in a bleak, heavily industrial landscape, like a steeltown outside of Chicago. Stanwyck and Douglas have long, pointed noses like daggers, shifty eyes, and permanent paranoia stemming from the murder. Heflin and Scott are skittish, always ready to jump, to get out of the way of the mainstream bullet train of life. They're definitely butterflies caught in the wheel, which people like Martha Ivers pay some poor soul to keep turning. Rain, smoke, dirty minds, and bad ideas make this a classic of the corrupt.

The Strange One

1957. Directed by Jack Garfein. Based on the novel *End as a Man* by Calder Willingham. Starring Ben Gazzara, Pat Hingle, George Peppard, and Mark Richman.

When I was a kid, parents of friends of mine used to threaten to send their sons to military school unless they behaved properly. My mother never held this possibility over my head, though, because she'd seen the adverse effect it had on my cousin who attended Culver Academy in Indiana. All it succeeded in doing was to make him meaner than he already was. My buddy Magic Frank was fascinated by *The Strange One,* and he convinced me to watch it after school one winter afternoon on television. "I'm Jocko DeParis!" Frank would snarl, in imitation of Ben Gazzara as the nasty cadet officer who specializes in making life miserable for plebes at the southern military academy to which they've all been condemned. My cousin and I once encountered the actor Vincent Price browsing art gallery windows off Michigan Avenue in Chicago one evening, and my cousin said to him, "I remember when you came to Culver and made a speech." Price nodded and grimaced. "Yes, indeed," he said. "I recall it well. How did you ever survive that prison?"

The military academy as presented in *The Strange One* is kind of a third-rate institution, a Citadel or VMI-like bastion of retrograde thought and racist behavior. Gazzara's Jocko is an evil madman, a manipulator of the weak, a megalomaniac of whom most of the cadets are afraid. Jocko's malevolent leer has everyone weirded out, but they're powerless to avoid him. They hate his guts, of course, especially when he's responsible for a cadet's death; and the ending is justifiably bizarre when the others gang up on Jocko and ride him out of town, literally on a rail. "You can't do this to me!" shouts Gazzara, hanging off the end of the train. "I'm Jocko DeParis!"

This dark vision of military academy life is chock full of homosexual overtones, later to surface in *Dress Gray* (1985) in all its glory-hole glory. But *The Strange One* was a great response to John Ford's paean to West Point, *The Long Gray Line* (1955), which used Tyrone Power and Maureen O'Hara, along with Ward Bond and Donald Crisp, to evoke a dreamlike nobility about academy life. Nothing sordid at The Point, of course; only at a low-rent institution could events like those depicted in *The Strange One* occur. In fact, this was an extremely brave little movie, and Gazzara's performance is a *tour de force.* Pat Hingle, too, distinguished himself mightily. I remember thinking when I first saw it that there had to be a great deal of truth in *The Strange One,* and that there were a lot of Jocko DeParises out in the world. As the years passed and I got further out among the planet's population, I ran into more than a few Jockos; and thanks in part to this movie, I knew how to recognize them right away, and managed to avoid as many as I could. Unfortunately, I'm still having to avoid them.

The Stranger

1946. Directed by Orson Welles. Starring Orson Welles, Loretta Young, Richard Long, and Edward G. Robinson.

The darkness of the soul is under scrutiny here. Welles directs himself as an escaped Nazi commander, Franz Kindler, living in disguise as a New England college professor. Government agents free a toady of Welles's in Europe and tail him on his route to his former superior. Edward G. shadows the nervous little mouse-man to a peaceful Connecticut town, early fall, leaves blown along the streets under a retreating sun. A blissful little town, it seems. Who would think of looking for a Nazi monster in such a place?

The genius of Welles is that he has virtually no trace of a German accent; he's able to pull off the deception completely. He's engaged to Loretta Young, the college president's daughter; he's a popular professor, and his eccentricities—his pet project is repairing the town clock on the church face—are accepted. After all, what New Englander isn't slightly off-kilter him- or herself? The only person who doesn't care for Welles is Young's brother, Noah, played by Richard Long. There's just something about Welles that strikes Noah the wrong way; and eventually it's Noah whom Edward G. enlists to aid him in the exposure and capture of Welles. But Welles is a brilliant guy; he kills the little rat who led Robinson to the town, burying him under a

pile of leaves in the woods. Then Welles kills Loretta's Irish set-
ter, who insists on digging at the leaves. At first Welles and Robinson don't realize each other's real identities—Welles thinks
Robinson is just an antique dealer passing through. But one
night at dinner Welles reveals himself unwittingly to Robinson.
During a discussion about the war, politics, and so on, someone
mentions Karl Marx in the context of German thought. "Yes,"
says Welles, "but Marx was not a German, he was a Jew."

In the middle of the night Edward G. wakes suddenly: Marx
was not a German, he was a Jew! Welles is the Nazi! Now Robinson begins to spin his own web around Welles, to try to force his
hand. The chase culminates in a spectacular scene on the clock
tower, where Welles has gone to work on the damaged springs.
During this scene I always think of Graham Greene's wonderful
statement from *The Third Man* (also, of course, a great Orson
Welles movie): "In Italy for thirty years under the Borgias they
had warfare, terror, murder, bloodshed. But they produced Mi-
chelangelo, Leonardo da Vinci, and the Renaissance. In Switzer-
land they had brotherly love. They had five hundred years of
democracy and peace. And what did that produce? The cuckoo
clock."

The idea of a monster in our midst is not new and not fantasy, either. There are lots of them. And if it hadn't been for
some quirk of fate, the monster would be you or me. And what
makes us so certain we're not? The horror perpetrated by the
Nazis is second to none in the annals of recorded history, and
Welles brilliantly portrays Franz Kindler as corruption and evil
personified. But there's a larger component to his madness: the
unwavering, granite-hard belief that *he is right.*

Stranger on the Third Floor

1940. Directed by Boris Ingster. Starring John McGuire, Peter Lorre, Margaret
Tallachet and Elisha Cook, Jr.

This is a wild, short piece of neo-Expressionist terror-noir. Ingster makes America look like Eastern Europe at its darkest hour

with the story of half-hunk/half-wimp reporter McGuire, who comes upon the slain body of Nick, proprietor of a diner across the street from McGuire's roominghouse, with Elisha Cook, Jr., kneeling over the corpse. McGuire testifies at Cook's trial, attended by snoozing jurors and presided over by a senile, distracted judge. Despite Cook's heart-rending protests of his innocence, the judge and jury send him to the electric chair. McGuire is haunted by Cook's screams and the fact that he did not actually see Cook kill Nick. McGuire's girlfriend, Margaret Tallachet, bolts from the courtroom, upset that McGuire is even involved, convinced that their relationship is ruined, that they'll be forever cursed by Cook's conviction.

McGuire goes back to his lonely bed-sitting room, where he's terrorized by a neighbor, a nasty old man who keeps McGuire awake with his snoring, and by the landlady, who insists that McGuire's typewriting is disturbing her and the bald creep snorer. "He's been here fourteen years and never missed a rent payment!" she says of the snorer. "Every week!" the old bird adds. McGuire is frustrated, callow, uncertain, alone. He hates his neighbor, and mentions to a fellow newspaperman that he'd kill him if he had the guts and the chance. "I'd like to slit his throat," McGuire says.

One evening McGuire notices a weird-looking guy with bug eyes, thick lips and crazed expression, wearing a long white scarf, sitting on the steps of his roominghouse. Later that night he spies the stranger ducking into the bathroom on the third floor of the house itself before running back down into the street when he thinks McGuire has gone back into his room. McGuire has a bizarre dream, which is the highlight of the movie. Presented in pounding Prussian delirium, this nightmare relentlessly torments McGuire, with Cook, the neighbor and everyone he knows turning against him. Of course, in real life, the neighbor has been murdered, his throat cut, and we know the madman, played by Peter Lorre, who doesn't say a word in the movie until it's more than halfway finished, has killed the guy. We realize, too, along with McGuire, that Lorre murdered

Nick in the diner. Now it's up to McGuire to prove Cook's innocence before they fry him, and also to prove to the cops that he, McGuire, didn't slice up the snorer.

Following Lorre's success as the child-murderer in Fritz Lang's classic *M*, made in Germany in 1931, he was brought to the States where he kept being cast as an insane killer. It took awhile before Hollywood realized he could do anything else. The thing is that he played these crazed butchers so well, appearing so convincingly deranged, that the typecasting is understandable. In this, he's an escaped mental patient, and it's up to McGuire's girlfriend to identify him as the fiend. Lorre's scarf is borrowed, along with glazed look, from Conrad Veidt's somnambulist creeper Césare in Robert Wiene's 1919 *Cabinet of Dr. Caligari*. Ingster's expressionist style comes from the Wiene/Dreyer/Murnau branch of Grimm's Gargoyle Academy. Combined with the cheap set ambience of shadowy streets, mean circumstances and narrow minded America of the late 1930s—(Is it any different now? Or ever?)—the picture is solidly sinister. Despite some bad acting (especially by McGuire), and dumb dialogue, *Stranger on the Third Floor* ranks right up there with Val Lewton's dark corners of the cinematic mind.

Of course, once Lorre's nailed, things are hunky-dory again with McGuire and his gal, and Elisha Cook, Jr., is sprung, appearing at the end as a cabbie giving the happy couple a lift. One hopes McGuire and wife will find a more suitable place to live.

Strangers on a Train

1951. Directed by Alfred Hitchcock. Screenplay by Raymond Chandler and Czenzi Ormonde; adapted by Whitfield Cook. Based on a novel by Patricia Highsmith. Starring Farley Granger, Robert Walker, Ruth Roman, Leo G. Carroll, Patricia Hitchcock, and Marion Lorne.

This is as good as it gets. Hitchcock made the Hall of Fame for this picture, taking a clumsily written but superbly plotted book by Highsmith (her first novel) and pitching a perfect game, right down to the googly-eyed carny oldtimer crawling through the mud and dirt under the out-of-control roller ride at the end. It all clicks, and there are great performances by virtually everyone.

Tennis champ Guy (Granger) meets richkid psychopath Bruno (Walker) on a train where Bruno entertains Guy with a wild, wicked idea: What if they each murdered the other's nemesis? Who would know? How could they ever be linked together, two strangers on a train? Guy laughs it off, but to get the crazy Bruno away from him—soon realizing Bruno is bonkers—he says yeah, let's do it. Bruno, of course, takes this seriously.

Guy wants his first wife, a nasty bitch, to divorce him so that he can marry a rich girl who's also pretty and nice; Bruno wants Guy to kill his father, and elicits from Guy the information that he'd prefer it if his wife were out of the way. Naturally, Bruno does the job, his part of the "bargain," and presses Guy to do likewise. Bruno turns up at the same social affairs Guy's at, freaking Guy out. At first Guy's new girlfriend's dad, Leo G. Carroll, and the girl, Ruth Roman, are entertained by Bruno— but soon they see he's nuts, too, and Guy finds out Bruno's done away with his wife. Bruno's strangled her at an amusement park, on a boat ride, and he's furious that Guy won't reciprocate. There's a showdown at the park and the madman is vanquished, as per the movie morality code—but the evil remains, staining everyone involved.

It's Robert Walker who takes this movie. His deranged Bruno is absolute in his torment and mania. His suffering is brutal, he's filled with incredible pain and sadness. Marion Lorne does a great job as his doting mother, giving us the classic mama's boy routine. Nothing's bolted down in Bruno's brain; his head is like a trashed pinball machine, with little sparks and bulbs lighting up here and there but in all the wrong places and sequences. Utterly depraved, he can say anything at anytime to anybody; it's a great, great role. Granger's decency is belied by his hypocrisy: who wouldn't want the roadblock to a better life removed noiselessly and painlessly? Laura Elliot, as Guy's sluttish wife, makes it seem O.K. for Guy to go ahead and strangle her himself; we won't mind. My question is: Why is Guy so convinced Ruth Roman will work out any better? Just because she has good manners and money? So does Bruno! The trick here is that there's a story that follows this story. Take a good look around: nobody's perfect.

Suddenly

1954. Directed by Lewis Allen. Starring Frank Sinatra, Sterling Hayden, James Gleason, and Nancy Gates.

Before Sinatra made his comeback in 1953 as Maggio in *From Here to Eternity*, arrested is about the only thing he could get in Hollywood. After Maggio, for which performance he won the Academy Award, Sinatra was besieged by producers and directors begging him to star in their movies. That he chose *Suddenly* as his initial vehicle is not so strange to understand, considering the political climate of the day. It was smack dab in the middle of the McCarthy Era, and *Suddenly* is a fiercely patriotic flick; Sinatra was eager to ingratiate himself further—and forever—with the powers that prevailed.

Suddenly, California, is a small town where nothing much out of the ordinary happens. Sterling Hayden is the sheriff, Nancy Gates is the woman he loves, and James Gleason is her father, a retired Secret Service man. Nancy's a widow—her husband was killed in the war—and her little boy idolizes Hayden; he wants to carry a gun just like him and kill all the bad guys. The movie is peppered with pro-American, anti-Communist comments. Sterling Hayden's idea of a date with Nancy Gates is to ask her if he can take her to church on Sunday.

The President of the United States decides to stop over in Suddenly on his way to Los Angeles to do a little fishing. A special train carrying Eisenhower or a reasonable facsimile is due to arrive at five P.M., and nobody knows about it except for

Hayden. A group of Secret Service men show up, the leader of whom, Carney, formerly worked for Nancy's father. He wants to see the old guy and Hayden agrees to drive him up to the house, which overlooks the arrival platform of the train station.

Meanwhile, Frank Sinatra and his boys have already taken over the house, the perfect place from which to take a pop at the President when he detrains. Posing as FBI agents, they con their way in but are shortly revealed for what they really are: hired killers being paid a half-million dollars to assassinate the Chief. There's an airplane waiting nearby to take them out of the country as soon as it's done. After Hayden and Carney arrive, there's a shoot-out; Carney's killed and Hayden's wounded in the arm. Sinatra brags that he won a Silver Star during the war for offing twenty-seven Germans. But Hayden taunts him, fingering Frankie for a psycho, a Section Eight reject who was discharged early because he liked killing too much. "Yeah," says Frank, "I did a lot of chopping over there, a lot of chopping."

Everybody bugs Sinatra about his lack of patriotism. How could a former infantryman, a Silver Star hero like himself, assassinate the President? How can he justify it? It won't make any difference at all, Frank explains. Five minutes after he shoots the President, there'll be a new one. "And I'll have half a million bucks." But of course things go wrong. One of Frankie's goons is spotted in town and shot dead. A television repairman shows up at the house, having been called earlier by old Pop Gleason, and he proceeds to electrocute another of Sinatra's men while the bad guy's setting the sight on the highpowered rifle propped up on a table by the window.

Sinatra's the last one left and he manages to knock down Hayden and Gleason and grab the rifle precisely at five o'clock, but the train doesn't stop: it barrels right through Suddenly. The Secret Service radioed for it to go on by as soon as the stranger, Sinatra's man, was discovered. There's a final shoot-out at the house—the kid finds old Pop's gun in his top dresser drawer— and Hayden blasts Frankie for good. We know that now Nancy will agree to accompany Hayden to church.

Suddenly is an odd little movie, rarely seen, almost a trifle. But Sinatra's performance is intense and true, worth shifting your weight through the Red Scare crapola patched into the script to pacify the HUAC buzzards. Frank even sports his "Come Fly With Me" brim, but he doesn't snap his fingers once.

Sunset Boulevard

1950. Directed by Billy Wilder. Starring William Holden, Gloria Swanson, Erich von Stroheim, Nancy Olson, and Jack Webb.

It's tough to write about *Sunset Boulevard* without treading on ground already covered by film historians. This movie is the definitive statement on Dream Factory *noir*. Wilder's story is a Gothic, poetic essay on the dark side of the Hollywood moon. A once-famous actress, Norma Desmond, exquisitely and chillingly acted by Gloria Swanson, herself a former silent screen star, is a multi-millionairess holed up in her Hollywood mansion with no companion save her butler-chauffeur Max von Mayerling. Max is also a relic of the industry, having been a director as well as Norma Desmond's first husband. Still devoted to her, Max, played with grand Prussian forebearance by von Stroheim, works hard at protecting Norma, writing her dozens of phony fan letters each day in an effort to make her think that she's still popular, still remembered by an adoring public.

Into Norma's bizarre arena stumbles an out-of-work, flat busted screenwriter named Joe Gillis (William Holden). Gillis replaces Norma's recently deceased pet chimpanzee as the immediate object of her affection. She "hires" him to help her rewrite her script of *Salomé*, which she intends as her comeback vehicle. In the absence of any better offers, Joe becomes Norma's kept man. Norma knows what she wants; she's obsessed with herself, with the resumption of her career, and out of respect for her past accomplishments she's humored and treated tenderly by such a still-luminous figure as Cecil B. DeMille.

The casting in this is marvelous: besides Swanson and von

Stroheim, other early motion picture stars like Buster Keaton, Anna Q. Nilsson and H. B. Warner make appearances. Von Stroheim's Max is particularly affecting; his devotion to the deluded Desmond is heartbreaking, his respect for her unassailably sincere. And Holden's Joe Gillis is played with the perfect degree of spinelessness; he's the cynical but weak-willed dreamer whose lack of self-respect is responsible for his finding himself floating facedown dead in Norma's swimming pool. It's from this prone and posthumous posture that Gillis narrates his story, a device that serves to lend an eerier-than-usual aspect to the proceedings. Tales told by dead men are usually worth listening to, and this one is no exception.

Joe breaks free now and again, sparks briefly with his (absent) buddy Jack Webb's girlfriend, but returns to Norma, weak coward that he is. When Joe finally feels he can't go any lower and strides purposefully out the door, Norma shoots him and he bellyflops into the pool. Norma's madness is in full flower now, and she stretches out as Max coaxes her downstairs amidst a horde of cops, reporters, and photographers, with gossip columnist Hedda Hopper describing the action, by pretending he's directing her in a scene from *Salomé*.

The movie is an arrow straight into the heart of the Hollywood mystique. It's something beyond aberration, a larger remark which may not be literature but is nevertheless serious and quite profound.

They Made Me a Criminal

1939. Directed by Busby Berkeley. Starring John Garfield, Claude Rains, Gloria Dickson, Ann Sheridan, May Robson, and The Dead End Kids.

Claude Rains gets to play Javert to Garfield's Jean Valjean, and does it beautifully. Garfield is Johnny Bradfield, the middleweight champ. On the night he defeats a challenger for his title there's a drunken brawl at his apartment, and a newspaperman who threatened to expose Johnny for the party animal that he is—blowing his mom-and-apple-pie-in-the-kitchen image—is murdered. His manager and girlfriend split and crack up on the highway. Both are killed and burned beyond recognition. The manager is wearing Johnny's watch so the cops think it's Bradfield who's dead. In the meantime, the reporter's body is found but Johnny gets away without anyone seeing him. He goes to see his unscrupulous lawyer who advises Johnny to get out of town and never come back. Never fight again, never use his cockeyed southpaw boxing stance. Johnny asks for his ten thousand bucks stashed in the lawyer's safe. The lawyer gives him ten bucks instead and tells him to get lost or he'll spill the beans and say Johnny aced the reporter. Johnny thinks he did it, too, but it was the manager who cracked the guy in the head with a bottle; Johnny was drunk, passed out, and didn't see what happened. Now that everyone thinks it was Johnny who died in the car crash he can escape, but he's got to change his name, his identity. He becomes a road tramp named Jimmy Dolan.

Rains is a discredited detective: he once fingered and arrested a guy who went to the chair for murder, and then the real killer confessed. So now all Rains gets to cover is the morgue beat. He's ridiculed by the other cops. He's not convinced it's Johnny Bradfield who died in the wreck, though, and he starts digging into the case. Garfield—né Bradfield now Dolan—hoboes his way back and forth and up and down around the country. He winds up in Arizona, bearded, sick, beaten down, broke. He stumbles onto a farm run by Gloria Dickson and her mother, May Robson; The Dead End Kids work on the place, imported from the Lower East Side of New York for rehabilitation, like an honor work-farm for boys. Garfield collapses and the women nurse him back to health. When he recovers he helps take care of the place and pals around with Billy Halop, Bobby Jordan, Huntz Hall, and the rest of the gang, teaching them to box, of course. There's a scary scene where they all go for a swim in an irrigation tank and almost drown when a farmer lets the water drain, halfway from the top, not knowing anybody was foolish enough to go swimming in it. But Garfield gets them out.

The farm needs money to keep going, and the kids convince Garfield to enter himself in a boxing contest where he has to go three rounds with a light heavy to win five hundred dollars. At first Garfield refuses, but when he sees he's let everyone down he agrees to try it. At the weigh-in a local photographer takes a picture of him with his left fist reared back in the unorthodox Bradfield style, and of course Claude Rains spots the photo in a newspaper 2,500 miles away. He takes off for Arizona right away, sure it's Johnny Bradfield in the fuzzy photo. Again he's ridiculed by the other cops, but he doesn't mind now: he *knows* he's right.

Rains gets to the arena just in time. Garfield comes in and spots Rains, whom he remembers from New York. When Rains calls, "Hello, Johnny!" Garfield knows he's got to cover up, so he decides to fight righthanded, not his usual southpaw. As a result, he gets beaten to a pulp for two-and-a-half rounds, but stays on his feet. Gloria and her mother and the kids beg Garfield to quit, but he won't, he can't, and at the last he switches suddenly to his left-hand stance and pulverizes the brutish pug. He wins the dough for the farm and prepares to be cuffed by Rains and taken back to the Big Town to be tried for murder. But Rains relents; he can't take Johnny back—not after witnessing him suffer that horrible beating, sacrificing himself for the sake of his friends. Just as Javert drowns himself in *Les Misérables* rather than arrest Monsieur Madeleine, Rains returns emptyhanded to New York, prepared to accept a lifetime of further abuse from his fellow policemen. "I was wrong," he tells them. "Johnny Bradfield is dead." Now all Rains has to do is hang on for his pension.

This is a sentimental sucker punch of a movie, but one with a straightforward recognition of man's inhumanity to man. And great scenes with Garfield running from a railroad bull on the tops of boxcars with the train moving, bloody boxing matches, and the usual Dead End Kids' antics. Fastmoving, Depression-era melodrama with credit to Victor Hugo.

They Won't Believe Me

1947. Directed by Irving Pichel. Screenplay by Jonathan Latimer. Starring Robert Young, Susan Hayward, Jane Greer, Rita Johnson, and Tom Powers.

Cast against type as a womanizing, greedy heel who's married Rita Johnson for her money, Robert Young, a desultory stockbroker, takes up with pretty little Jane Greer, whom he informs on one of their eleven consecutive Saturday afternoons together, that he is going to leave his wife and marry. Jane has arranged to be transferred by her firm to Montreal from New York, and Young agrees to entrain with her that night, right after he spills the news to Rita. The wife listens to him as he packs, remains calm, then tells him that she's purchased a stock brokerage firm for him in LA, along with a fabulous house, and when next we see the faithless Young he's waking up on a train all right, but in a sleeper compartment rattling toward the west coast, not the frozen north.

His habits don't change in the yellow light and air of Los Angeles. He soon begins a romance with a secretary played by Susan Hayward. She's slick, sexy and smart, and assists Young in the business. Young promises her he'll leave Rita but when Rita buys an isolated ranch in the mountains he goes with her. After a while in the wilderness, Young goes stir crazy and contacts Hayward. He rendez-vous with her in LA and together they drive toward Reno, where Young intends to divorce Rita and marry Hayward. Their car goes off the road and smashes up, burning Susan Hayward's body beyond recognition. The cops too hastily conclude that it's Rita who's dead and Young, recovering from his own injuries in a hospital, does not move to disabuse them of their belief.

On his return to the ranch, Young discovers that Rita has killed herself. The body has not been discovered, so he dumps it in a nearby lake. Her fortune is now his, and he takes off on an idle ramble through the tropics. In Jamaica he bumps into Jane Greer, his old flame, and they resume their romance, though of course she puts him through a few hoops owing to the fact that he'd crossed her back in New York. In reality, she's working for the cops who mean to fry him for the murder of Susan Hayward, who has disappeared altogether. They've never figured out that it was Hayward who died in the crash, not Rita Johnson.

Greer snares Young and leads him back to LA, where he's arrested and put on trial. He explains to the jury what's happened, not attempting to paint himself as any sort of good guy, misunderstood or otherwise. He admits that he's guilty of "many derelictions but not murder." Young relates his sordid story while on the witness stand, and we watch it all unfold in flashback. He grimaces and sweats as he tells the truth for a change, the one thing that can make him sweat. He's been such a rotten guy that despite his innocence of the charge Young's convinced the jurors will hang him. While they're out deliberating, he jumps from a courtroom window to his death. The jury enters and pronounces him not guilty.

Young is great as the squirrelly sonofabitch philanderer, and Hayward and Greer do their work cleanly and one-dimensionally as required. But Rita Johnson, as the ever giving and forgiving wife, takes the honors here. She has a bland, deceptive approach, which catches both her husband and the viewer off-guard, delivering much more than at first seems apparent. Her face hides hurt or happiness until precisely the right moment to divulge her true feelings. She is a benevolent manipulator but a woman who somehow cannot let this man go, which is her fateful flaw, her one weakness. To have a weakness of such magnitude for such a weak cad is finally, she recognizes, so far beneath her, beneath what she knows to be honorable and correct, that she decides she is unable to live with herself. Too long, too wrong, sad song.

Thieves' Highway

1949. Directed by Jules Dassin. Screenplay by A. I. Bezzerides, based on his novel *Thieves' Market*. Starring Richard Conte, Lee J. Cobb, Valentina

Cortesa, Jack Oakie, Joseph Pevney, Barbara Lawrence, David Opatoshu, and Millard Mitchell.

Bezzerides was one of the promising proletarian writers of the 1930s and '40s; his fiction appeared in *Scribner*'s magazine, stories like the one *Thieves' Highway* is based on. By the 1950s he was a veteran of *noir*, writing screenplays like *They Drive By Night* (1940) and *Kiss Me Deadly* (1955). *Thieves' Highway* is a typical proletarian melodrama that pits one earnest man against an exploitative, corrupt businessman attempting to control a marketplace.

In this case it's the San Francisco/Oakland produce market (scenes were shot on both sides of the Bay, and on the road from Santa Rosa to San Francisco and Oxnard). Richard Conte, in a rare sympathetic, heroic role, plays a recently discharged soldier who comes home and finds that his once-strong father is permanently crippled from a big rig accident (the truck, we learn, was purposefully sabotaged by a produce market boss), so Conte has to take his savings from the service and buy an old truck in order to support his parents and get a new stake to marry his girl. He hooks up with a pal of his dad's and on his first run with a load of apples has an accident while fixing a flat. Ed, his partner, helps him out, and follows Conte in his own truck, unaware that he is being tailed by two goons from the produce market who work for the same guy that was responsible for Conte's father's accident.

Conte arrives in San Francisco and leaves his rig in front of the warehouse of a wholesale merchant named Figlia, played by Lee J. Cobb. Unbeknownst to Conte, Cobb is the unscrupulous guy who shagged his old man, and whose thugs run Ed off the road on his way to town, killing him and wrecking his truck because Ed refuses to deal with them anymore. Conte doesn't know this yet, of course, so he allows himself to be lured to the apartment of a sexy foreign chick named Rica, to rest up from the road. While he's relaxing at Rica's (who's been paid by Cobb to keep Conte occupied), Cobb sells all of the apples in Conte's load. When Conte returns to Figlia's and finds out what Cobb's done, he demands that Cobb hand over the money. Cobb gives it to him but sends two of his boys after Conte, who rob him; Rica takes the cash and tries to get away but the goons grab her and take it back. Conte's convinced Rica's in with the bad guys but she swears she was doing it for him. Conte's fiancée, Polly, locates Conte at Rica's apartment, sees that something's up between them, hears about Conte's losing his stake, and splits forever; he's of no use to her now.

Conte then goes back to Cobb's warehouse, finds out about Ed's death and that Cobb has gone to salvage Ed's load. He gets the lowdown on Cobb from a disaffected heavy of his, that Cobb has been using the independent drivers against each other and is responsible for many "accidents" of uncooperative drivers. Conte finds Cobb at a roadside diner and begins beating on him like a maniac, forcing Cobb to return his money. The cops come and pull him off, and Conte heads back to San Francisco, to Rica, who all of a sudden looks a lot better to him than the gutless, fairweather bitch Polly.

Writer Bezzerides brings in the immigrant touch in the form of Conte's Greek-American parents and Rica's dark, European, heavily accented refugee (Valentina Cortesa in her first American film role, later to resurface in François Truffaut's *Day For Night*); the indy trucker versus the mob-type wholesaler king; plays off the Ideal American WASP Country Club Shallow Spoiled Piece against the Mysterious Foreign Girl trying to make her lonely way in the new world; the honest GI opposed to the stateside slackers. Director Dassin was another one on the Hollywood commie list (he married actress and later Greek political official Melina Mercouri), and this movie shows why.

Tom Horn

1980. Directed by William Wiard. Screenplay by Tom McGuane and Bud Shrake. Starring Steve McQueen, Linda Evans, Richard Farnsworth, Billy Green Bush, and Slim Pickens.

A vastly underrated, uncelebrated, and seldom-seen movie, *Tom Horn* is based on the autobiography of an enforcer in the Wyoming–Montana cattle country of the late 19th century. McQueen, in his next-to-last film, portrays Horn as a softspoken, unassuming rustler eliminator, hired by rancher Farnsworth to find and, if necessary, knock off the boys who are stealing his and others' beef on the hoof. This is illegal, of course, so Horn is actually paid by a consortium of local ranchers on the sly. He does his job, is apprehended by the authorities, and is put on trial for murder.

Steve McQueen was perfect at playing the stoic, tight-lipped victim, and Tom Horn is not very much different than his roles as Josh Randall in the T.V. series *Wanted: Dead or Alive*, *The Cincinnati Kid*, or Doc McCoy in *The Getaway*, etc. It's McQueen, limited but effective. Tom Horn was the ideal role for him. Along the way he gets involved with a pretty schoolteacher played by Linda Evans, whose husky voice, lovely blue eyes and ash-blonde hair semisweep him away. An interesting touch is her telling him about her life in Hawaii, which seems a thoroughly exotic place to someone out riding the Montana range every day. Their relationship is handled well except for a few elliptical love scenes tossed in at the insistence of the studio. This is not a mush movie.

The dirty part here is that the ranchers who hired Horn in the first place don't come forward to back him up once he's arrested and taken into custody. Nobody defends him at the trial, and Horn keeps his mouth shut. I don't know if McQueen knew yet that he was dying of cancer, but it's as if he knows there's nothing he can do, so why cry about it. He does attempt to escape from the jailhouse once, but doesn't get too far. Slim Pickens plays the deputy at the jail, a reprise of his role in *One-Eyed Jacks*, where Marlon Brando fakes him out and gets away. So McQueen tightens his lips, doesn't really respond when Farnsworth makes an attempt to convey his sympathy, sucks it all in. He hangs and it's horrible and worthless, though he is a paid killer.

This is a quiet film that shows hypocrisy and betrayal in full light. Horn's character is given strength by an intelligent script; no McGuane jokes à la *Rancho Deluxe* or *Missouri Breaks,* no "The further north you go, the more things eat your horse." If this script were updated and set in rainy 1940s San Francisco, or sleazy 1980s New York, it would be hailed as superb *noir.* As it is, it's fair enough, with the same truth-or-consequences jolts, underhanded behavior, and low-key tough nut (anti-) hero. Not only that but it's a good movie to look at, too. Nobody comes off clean here; only the scenery is unpolluted. This is a deeper and harder story than it seems; it's muted, that's all. No picnic at the beach.

Touch of Evil

1958. Directed by Orson Welles (who also wrote the screenplay). Starring Orson Welles, Charlton Heston, Marlene Dietrich, Janet Leigh, Akim Tamiroff, Joseph Calleia, Mercedes McCambridge, Dennis Weaver, and Zsa Zsa Gabor.

Welles is at his most imposing in this exhausting exercise in high-energy, self-conscious *noir.* The movie moves like Welles, slowly but with concentrated effort designed to maximize the result. And it works—almost unlike any other picture that so purposefully sets out to achieve a dark effect. Welles uses every trick in his book to make this a spooky case, but it still takes some indulgence and patience to allow the smoke to settle in all the right places.

The story gets tricky, but basically Welles, as Hank Quinlan, a detective on the California side of the Mexican border, decides to frame a guy named Sanchez, whom Welles is certain has murdered a man by installing a time bomb in his car, by planting evidence. Charlton Heston (Vargas), a Mexican detective on his honeymoon with his wife, Janet Leigh (Susan), gets involved in the case, figures out what Welles is doing, and tries to show Welles up for the crooked cop he is. Welles is famous for his frame jobs and Heston is a straight arrow, an idealist, the antithesis of Welles. Welles uses his toady, Menzies, to carry out his instructions, and Heston pushes him to get Welles. Welles has got a burn against lowlifes and criminals since he failed to pin a murder rap on the guy who killed his wife. He uses Akim Tamiroff, who looks like a Turkish Groucho Marx, to set up Vargas's wife, Susan, as a junkie in order to discredit Vargas. This is an especially fascinating scene, with Mercedes McCambridge playing a lesbian Mexican hoodlum, with the gang of wolf-eyed, leather-jacketed Mex punkers coming down like hyenas on the vulnerable blonde babe.

The movie is full of wild upsidedown and slanted camera angles (like Welles's *Mr. Arkadin*). It's shot in almost complete darkness; bodies move in and out of the light, their voices trail the action and are seemingly unconnected, unattached, to the phantom forms floating, hurtling, or lumbering through the camera frame. Marlene Dietrich chips in as a café fortune teller named Tanya, Welles's one friend of equal footing. Dennis Weaver has a great little scene as a fumbling, mumbling, nervous motel clerk cowed by the badgering Vargas. And Welles sneaks in cameos by Joseph Cotten, Joi Lansing, Keenan Wynn, and Zsa Zsa Gabor, as well as bits by a host of Mexican actors, all of whom combine to lend a circusy effect. Welles is gruff, fat, unshaven, addicted to bad cigars and candy bars. He understands what makes these criminals tick, not unlike a cop or sheriff in a Jim Thompson novel. It takes low-rent to trap low-rent.

Welles shot the movie in Venice, California, and managed to make it look like a San Diego/Tijuana borderland, mixing it skillfully with studio shots so that the landscape becomes an integral part of the entire scheme, almost like another character whose attitude and bearing forces others to modify their behavior. Welles is caught in a web because of Vargas's investigation into his unorthodox methods and kills Tamiroff in order to protect himself. Menzies, however, Welles's devoted aide, ends up betraying his boss to Vargas and is shot by Welles. Menzies then plugs Welles, who staggers down by the riverbank and collapses in a garbage heap. The righteous Vargas has done his job well, but he'll never be the presence Welles was. It turns out that the guy Welles framed for the bombing confesses to the crime, and Marlene makes the final judgment, saying, "He was a bad cop, but he was some kind of man." A purple prose movie, one with lots of—almost too much—character.

The Turning Point

1952. Directed by William Dieterle. Screenplay by Warren Duff, based on a story by Horace McCoy. Starring William Holden, Edmond O'Brien, Alexis Smith, Tom Tully, and Ed Begley.

Edmond O'Brien really knew how to play the victim, an unsuspecting customer of deceit, betrayal and unfortunate circumstances. He did it to a T in *D.O.A.* (1949) and he does it here as a crusading Estes Kefauver clone who heads up an investigative committee out to stymie mobsters but finds himself fodder for a bad cop who happens to be his own father, and a girlfriend who despite her best intentions falls for O'Brien's best pal. William Holden plays the bird-dogging buddy with the same self-contained and contain*ing* cynicism he brought to his role in *Sunset Boulevard* (1950).

I never did care much for Alexis Smith's looks, couldn't really buy her as an object of gentlemen's desire other than that she held some appeal as a well-to-do "handsome dame" (as Holden calls her here). Anyway, she's working for O'Brien and Holden is a reporter for the *Chronicle* who digs up the dirt on his boyhood friend's dad and has to tell him the sad truth. Alexis resists Holden at first, knows she's attracted to him but isn't certain what side he's on. Tom Tully (later of *San Francisco Beat/The Lineup*) plays the cop-pop who ends up dead while trying to right himself for the sake of his son. He was the classic gruff Irishman, a decent enough guy who can't really be blamed for looking for a few extra bucks as he turns forty-plus and wants the best for his wife and kid. And Ed Begley became the consummate schemer with this picture, continuing the role right into *Odds Against Tomorrow* (1959). He plays the big mob boss, Eichelberger, who controls the rackets in a midwestern city. Force is his forte; muscle, murder and arson are his aces; he's an amoral monster, willing to torch babies in order to stay on top.

The interesting feature here is that it's O'Brien who survives despite the crushing revelation of his father's dishonesty, the object of his romantic affection defecting to buddy Bill, and the ultimate ineffectuality of the investigative hearings. Horace McCoy, whose story upon which the movie was based, novelized and published it in 1959 under the title, *Corruption City*. It's not much of a novel, not compared to McCoy's *They Shoot Horses, Don't They* and *I Should Have Stayed Home* (maybe the ultimate anti-Hollywood story), but I never have forgotten his line about getting away from it all, going up to a lake in Canada and walking across on the backs of fish.

Vera Cruz

1954. Directed by Robert Aldrich. Starring Gary Cooper, Burt Lancaster, Denise Darcel, Cesar Romero, Jack Elam, Ernest Borgnine, and Charles Buchinsky (Bronson).

This is the movie that immortalized for me Burt Lancaster's smile: those 108 give-or-take-a-few giant gleaming teeth frozen in time that Burt first used to such advantage in *The Crimson Pirate* (1952). In *Vera Cruz,* the deeply tanned and handsome Lancaster wore a dusty black outfit and black drawstring hat, a black leather wristband and a silver-studded black gunbelt with a pearl-handled revolver strapped to his right thigh. He's an outlaw operating in Maximilian's Mexico who hooks up with Coop, playing a former Confederate Colonel from Louisiana who has no desire to live under Yankee rule. Coop's idea is to score enough loot to re-finance the Rebel cause.

Burt makes a superb gunslinger, especially when he mows

down two thugs with a classy backhanded move. He and Coop and their gang—a greasy bunch of javelinas led by Borgnine, Bronson and evil-eyed Elam—join up with Maximilian rather than Benito Juarez because the Emperor pays better, and agree to aid in escorting a French countess, Denise Darcel, and her carriage to Vera Cruz. The trick, of course, is that a shipment of gold is hidden in the carriage, and everybody wants it. One of Juarez's generals, Ramirez, pulls a nice stunt when he surrounds Burt and his men on the walls of a town square. Burt rotates his head as dozen after dozen of Ramirez's peasant army appear, and when Lancaster sees he's trapped he unleashes his magnificent grin and the world stops, blinded by the glare.

Director Aldrich (*Kiss Me Deadly*, *Autumn Leaves*, etc.) has his cinematographer, Ernest Laszlo, track the procession of lancers and gunmen from the tops of Indian pyramids along the road, shots reminiscent of Zoltan Korda's *Four Feathers* (1939) or *King of the Khyber Rifles* (Henry King, 1953). Bernardo Bertolucci might owe a debt to Aldrich due to the similarity of the final scene set-up with the woman in the window half-angled following the gunfight in the street; the way Darcel looks away from Cooper is echoed in Bertolucci's *Before the Revolution*.

Burt's name is Joe Erin; Coop is Ben Train. Joe is slick, crude, flashy, schooled by old Ace Hannah, the man who gunned down Joe's dad; and Joe makes a point of telling Ben how and when Joe paid Ace back. Ben Train is elegant, older, gentler. Joe says of Ben: "I don't trust him. He likes people; you can never count on a man like that." Joe spills wine on himself when he drinks from a glass; Ben speaks French (New Orleans, you know) and charms the countess to Joe's dismay. They make a great team.

Vera Cruz, despite its Hollywood veneer, retains a ragged edge, the same feel you get from reading John Reed's *Insurgent Mexico*, his reportage from the Mexican revolution. I pretended to be Joe Erin for months after seeing this. I was eight years old and loved to roll in the dirt shooting at Juaristas or the effete Austrian troops of Maximillian. Peckinpah's *Wild Bunch* (1969) has its roots in *Vera Cruz*, especially the final conflagration.

Burt gives his grandest grin as he plunges a lance into the throat of the Austrian commander. When he and Coop have their showdown, Burt twirls his pistol one last time into his holster before collapsing, grinning broadly, of course; the classic romantic tough guy gone but not forgotten, not by a long shot.

Where Danger Lives

1950. Directed by John Farrow. Screenplay by Charles Bennett; based on a story by Leo Rosten. Starring Robert Mitchum, Faith Domergue, Claude Rains, and Maureen O'Sullivan. Photography by Nicholas Musuraca.

This one's a little gem. Howard Hughes took over RKO studios in order to make a star out of Faith Domergue, who had been signed by Warner Brothers when she was sixteen. Hughes stole her away and figured he could do with her what he'd done with Jane Russell. But there was a difference—several differences, in fact—Jane had a fuller figure, which went over better at the time; a more pronounced profile; and a greater screen presence. As it turned out, Domergue did her best work in *Cult of the Cobra*, five years after this picture, and she was no longer a threat to Ava, Jane or any of the other brunette ballbusters. Hughes had shot this wad by then on Jean Peters, and Faith Domergue was a goner. The public never cottoned to her.

She was snakily seductive, though, and her reptilian eyebrows slither and squirm as she coils, strikes and collects Big Bob. Mitchum's a doctor who is dating his nurse (played by Maureen O'Sullivan, mostly behind a surgical mask, and who appears only briefly). One night a suicide attempt is wheeled in—Domergue—a black beauty who invites the Doc to her home the next night. She tells him she lives with her father (the boyfriend who brought her to the hospital splits immediately after she's checked in) and proceeds to wrap, roll and devour the new hunk. He forgets his nurse entirely—for the next few nights it's Cobra City, he's smitten and bitten. Then Margo (Faith's name) tells the Doc she has to leave town with her father and the fun is over. The Doc gets tipsy and busts in on Claude Rains, whom he thinks is Margo's pop, confesses his love and desire to marry her, all of which the bemused Claude drinks in without a blip beyond a raised eyebrow. Actually, there's lots of eyebrow raising in this movie: Domergue, Mitchum and Rains were all expert at one-eyebrow-upmanship, so for a while here it's kind of an eyebrow Olympics, with the three of them madly manipulating their respective forehead muscles.

Of course Claude's her husband, not her dad, and Margo goads them into a fight, which Mitchum wins, but not before the older guy whips him with a fireplace poker. The Doc pokes Claude, who collapses, and while Mitchum's out of the room, Nuestra Señora de las Culebras smothers her hubby with a pillow. She tells Mitchum when he returns that he's killed Claude, and they start running. Little does our good Doc know that she's a total wacko who's made multiple attempts at suicide, is something of a nymphomaniac, and a pathological liar who has not benefited from treatment by two or more of the country's foremost psychiatrists.

They drive from San Francisco south after spotting cops at the airport they think might be after them. Mitchum's muscles start seizing up—the poker-popping did some real damage to him, gave him a concussion so he keeps passing out, and his left hand goes dead, followed by his arm and ultimately his entire south side. The insane siren keeps pushing him, however, and they get trapped in a podunk town where they're forced to get married! I won't even go into this part of the story, it's too zany. Anyway, most of the action takes place at night, typical *noir* fare with great contrasts by Musuraca, tilted close-ups and devil-or-angel angles grabbing Domergue as she sheds her skins.

There's a *Touch of Evil*-like closure at the Mexican border, followed by Bob's rapprochement with the nurse, none of which counts. The thrill of this picture is Faith Domergue's Margo, her sick soul insinuating itself into Mitchum's inexperienced good doctor. This is a guy who hasn't been laid enough because he's been too busy studying, and when Domergue makes him think she's giving herself to him when in fact he's being sucked dry and made stupid by a voracious vampire whore, all we can do is shudder and be wary of love at first bite. (Doesn't have to be "love" of course—viz. *Fatal Attraction*, et al.)

My buddy Mike Swindle loves to repeat a line he heard from his friend Herman Ernest, Etta James's drummer, in New Orleans: "Broads—" Herman says, grinning and shaking his head, "ain't they a bargain, baby?"

White Heat

1949. Directed by Raoul Walsh. Starring James Cagney, Virginia Mayo, Steve Cochran, Margaret Wycherly, and Edmond O'Brien.

Momism at its finest. Cagney, as Cody Jarrett, is at his wigged-out best in this one. And Margaret Wycherly, as Ma Jarrett, is as powerful an influence on her boy as Mémêre Kerouac was on Jack. The Jarrett gang doesn't make a move until Cody clears the action with Ma. He gets migraine headaches and curls up at her feet, in her lap, throws himself into walls, on the bed. His wife, Virginia Mayo, hangs out all day in a silk slip, flirts with Steve Cochran, and when Cody has to do some time she takes up with the brute. Ma never liked her, anyway. Edmond O'Brien is the undercover cop who connives his way into the gang and leads Cody to disaster.

Cody is unparalleled as a bank robber, and he's tough as nails and twice as hard, a Dillinger. His soft spot is for his mom, and one of the great scenes in movie history comes when he's in prison and he learns she's died. He begins to moan, to shake, shudder, cry out in the mess hall. He gets up on the tables and crawls across the plates of food, knocking everything over. When the guards grab him he smashes them out of the way, spitting and sobbing and raging, uncontrollable. When he gets out of jail he goes after Cochran and Mayo, and they're scared shitless. They've seen Cody in action, know he shot one of the boys in cold blood after he was blinded by hot steam and was no longer useful. It was Ma taught him the ropes, forced him to be tough, the toughest. Only he keeps getting these damn headaches, the only thing that can bring him to his knees.

Cagney's portrayal of a psycho is different than any other. You can see the red liquid boiling behind his eyes, bubbling up and threatening to burst out of his skull. Mayo is the archetypal slut, vicious and cowardly; she'd sacrifice her baby sister to save herself. She's hot, though, slinky; and it's definitely a problem for Cody: he despises the side of himself that lusts after her. Cochran is the typical big lug goon, dressed in black shirts, white ties, and a large fedora; he's greasy, gorillalike. Mayo can pull him along on a chain, get him to hop for her pussy. But Cody's different: he's too crafty to get sucked in all the way, and as long as Ma's around to take care of the little things life is good; or as good as it gets for a fugitive.

O'Brien has a way of expressing fear that's totally believable. His big eyebrows lift and his face turns white, blank; he's always good. There are great weaselly little characters in stir; steady, hardnosed cops tracking Cody. There's a terrific part where the cops put a multicar tail on Ma, coordinated by radio. And she's a mean little lady, always dressed in black, Margaret Hamilton-Wicked Witch outfits. For as long as she's in it, this is Margaret Wycherly's movie, certainly her greatest role.

And the final scene, when Cody goes up in flames on the fuel tower "Made it Ma! Top of the World!" is orgasmic, wild, beautiful, and insane. Pure American nightmare.

The Wild One

1954. Directed by Laslo Benedek. Starring Marlon Brando, Mary Murphy, Lee Marvin, Robert Keith, and Jay C. Flippen.

This is one movie Brando apparently regrets ever having made. Why, precisely, I don't know, because it's a kick. Based on motorcycle-bum invasions of Hollister and Riverside, California, in the early 1950s, we get to see Marlon fairly bursting out of a pair of Levis, pretending to be the leader of a pack of wild and crazy shitkickers on a romp in a California town. Actually, Brando's mob are decent fellows compared to the group led by Lee Marvin, who steals the picture right, left, and up the middle. He's the real clown, no mistake about it. Brando, as Johnny, wears the slick, sleek leather jacket and gleaming-visored white and black cap; he's the cool cat. Marvin is the slob, the filthy, unshaven, striped T-shirt goon who scares people. You just know if he couldn't break a bottle over your head he'd break it over his own; a maniacal, grinning, low-rent loser audiences love. Brando is phony and pretentious, straining not to show his bourgeois roots.

In his novel *Sometimes A Great Notion*, Ken Kesey wrote very well about the GIs who mustered out of the service after World War Two and didn't want to go back to the straight life and so got on a Harley or an Indian and beat their way around the country, evolving into gangs like the Hell's Angels, Outlaws, Satan's Slaves, and so forth. The other side of the record formed the Motorcycle Association of America and rode around with their wives and kids on Sundays. The cats in the middle became cops, chasing down citizens on state highways.

Brando and the guys blow into the hick town and take over the downtown bar. Mary Murphy is the cute chick whose old man (read father) owns the place. She's attracted to Johnny and he takes her for a spin on his bike, makes out with her a little. She's roamy, anxious to take off for L.A., Frisco, somewhere; but she's a good girl and suppresses her animal instincts. Johnny knows he can knock her off if he wants to; but *he's* a good boy, not really like the others. Right. In truth, he doesn't know who he is; not this chubby boy in a leather carapace. The joint starts jumping when Marvin's bunch arrives. His gumbas are nasty suckers, the ones who spawned the Angels. They're dying to get at pretty little Mary and begin tearing the place apart. Marvin gets tossed in the local hoosegow for a bit but the townies can't control the mob. Brando has a trophy one of his cohorts copped for him from a motorcycle race, which he straps to the handlebars of his bike. No such straight regalia for Marvin's crew: these guys wear Nazi helmets, piss in their pants and on each other, and like it. Finally the state cops get called in and order is restored.

At the end Brando returns alone, zooms up to the bar, cuts the engine, and takes a seat at the end of the bar. Everybody's ready for him and his pals now. One wrong move and they'll cold cock him, put out his lights for good. But he takes out his stolen trophy and sets it on the bar for Mary Murphy; he's giving it to her, his gesture of affection and respect. It's too bad, he's saying, but no matter how square I really am on the inside, I just can't do it on the outside. No wife and kids in the suburbs for me, honey. You take this, keep it in your trunk, and look at it some lonely afternoon while the brats are napping and your husband's at work. Remember the slick oaf who cared enough to leave you be. A Real Romantic Gesture. Then he slides his fat fanny off the stool and waddles back out to his Harley, guns it up, and rides off into the sunset like a cool breeze.

Silly, ain't it?

Author's Note

Insofar as accuracy is concerned in the following, I guarantee only the veracity of the impression. I wrote these essays as I imagined many of the *Cahiers du Cinema* reviews of the 1950s were written, on the café or kitchen table at one in the morning. None have been revised for their publication in magazines. This is and was by design, in an effort to retain the freshness of the thought.

My thanks to those editors who first published many of these essays: Ed Gorman, Tommy Tompkins, Walter Bode, and Walter Donohue.

—B. G.

About the Author

Barry Gifford was born in 1946 in Chicago, Illinois, and was raised there and in Key West and Tampa, Florida. His novel *Wild at Heart* (made into an award-winning film by David Lynch) was the first in a succession of novels exploring a similar part of the American landscape that has brought him increasing acclaim. His books have been translated into twenty languages. One of them, *Night People*, was presented the Premio Brancati, Italy's national book award established by Pier Paolo Pasolini and Alberto Moravia. Mr. Gifford is also the author of *The Sinaloa Story*, *Port Tropique*, *Wyoming*, *Baby Cat-Face*, *My Last Martini*, *Perdita Durango*, and *The Wild Life of Sailor and Lula*, among other works of fiction. Screenplays include *Lost Highway* (with David Lynch), *Perdita Durango* (with Alex de la Iglesia), and *Hotel Room Trilogy*. He has published numerous books of poetry, including *Ghosts No Horse Can Carry* (Collected Poems 1967–1987), *Poems from Snail Hut*, *The Blood of the Parade*, *Persimmons: Poems for Paintings*, *Giotto's Circle*, *Beautiful Phantoms*, *Coyote Tantras*, and *Flaubert at Key West*. Works of nonfiction include *Bordertown* (with photographs by David Perry), *A Day at the Races*, *Jack's Book: An Oral Biography of Jack Kerouac* (with Lawrence Lee), and *The Phantom Father: A Memoir*. He lives in the San Francisco Bay Area.

Title List